HBJ Reading Program

Margaret Early

Bernice E. Cullinan
Roger C. Farr
W. Dorsey Hammond
Nancy Santeusanio
Dorothy S. Strickland

LEVEL 9

Telescopes

HBJ **HARCOURT BRACE JOVANOVICH, PUBLISHERS**
Orlando   San Diego   Chicago   Dallas

Acknowledgments

For permission to reprint copyrighted material, grateful acknowledgment is made to the following sources:

Atheneum Publishers, Inc.: "Until I Saw the Sea" from *I Feel the Same Way* by Lilian Moore. Text copyright © 1967 by Lilian Moore.

Cynthia Overbeck Bix: Adapted from "Floaters, Poppers, and Parachutes: Seeds That Travel" (Titled: "Floaters, Poppers, and Parachutes") by Cynthia Overbeck Bix. © 1984 by Cynthia Overbeck Bix.

Carolrhoda Books, Inc., 241 First Avenue North, Minneapolis, MN 55401: Adapted from *A Contest* by Sherry Neuwirth Payne. Copyright © 1982 by Carolrhoda Books, Inc.

Contemporary Books, Inc., Chicago, IL: "It Couldn't Be Done" from *The Collected Verse of Edgar A. Guest.* © 1934 by Contemporary Books, Inc.

Creative Arts Book Company: Adapted from *The Shoemaker's Gift,* interpreted by Lyndell Ludwig. Text copyright © by Lyndell Ludwig.

Delacorte Press: Adapted from *The Girl Who Knew It All* by Patricia Reilly Giff. Text copyright © 1979 by Patricia Reilly Giff.

Doubleday & Company, Inc.: "The Colors Live" from *Hailstones and Halibut Bones* by Mary Le Duc O'Neill. Copyright © 1961 by Mary Le Duc O'Neill.

E. P. Dutton, a division of New American Library: Adapted from *Do Not Open* by Brinton Turkle. Copyright © 1981 by Brinton Turkle.

Harcourt Brace Jovanovich, Inc.: Entries "dolly," "flipper," "giant," "gibbon," "gift," "giggle," "Gila monster," "gingersnap," "gingham," "giraffe," and "siding," the pronunciation key from p. 33 and 337, the short key from p. 35, and illustrations in *HBJ School Dictionary.* Copyright © 1985 by Harcourt Brace Jovanovich, Inc. From *HBJ Science,* Level Green, Grade 3 by Elizabeth K. Cooper et al. From *The Community: Living in Our World* by Paul E. Brandwein and Nancy W. Bauer. All published by Harcourt Brace Jovanovich, Inc.

Harper & Row, Publishers, Inc.: Illustrations from pp. 4, 7, 18, and 24 in *Chanticler and the Fox* from *The Canterbury Tales* by Geoffrey Chaucer, adapted and illustrated by Barbara Cooney. Copyright © 1958 by Harper & Row, Publishers, Inc. Published by Thomas Y. Crowell. Adapted from pp. 5–38 in *Eleanor Roosevelt* by Jane Goodsell. Copyright © 1970 by Jane Goodsell. Published by Thomas Y. Crowell. Abridged and adapted from "Family" in *The Boy Who Wanted a Family* by Shirley Gordon. Text copyright © 1980 by Shirley Gordon. Complete text, abridged and adapted, and illustrations from *THE GREAT BLUENESS and Other Predicaments,* written and illustrated by Arnold Lobel. Copyright © 1968 by Arnold Lobel. Slightly adapted excerpt from p. 52 in *The Kid Next Door and Other Headaches: Stories About Adam Joshua* by Janice Lee Smith. Text copyright © 1984 by Janice Lee Smith.

D. C. Heath and Company: "Trains at Night" from *The Packet* by Frances M. Frost.

The Instructor Publications, Inc., New York, NY 10017: "Face to Face" by Anita E. Posey and "My Star" by Marion Kennedy from *Poetry Place Anthology.* Copyright © 1983 by The Instructor Publications, Inc. Adapted from "Barbara Cooney's award-winning picture books . . . 'Make the World More Beautiful'" (Retitled: "Interview with Barbara Cooney") by Julia Smith from *Instructor* Magazine, March 1985. Copyright © 1985 by The Instructor Publications, Inc.

Lantern Press, Inc., Publishers: Adapted from *Matuk, The Eskimo Boy* by Vee Cawston. Copyright © 1965 by Vee Cawston.

Lerner Publications Company, 241 First Avenue North, Minneapolis, MN 55401; Adapted from "Adrift in Space" (Retitled: "In Space") in *Adrift in Space and Other Stories* by George Zebrowski. Copyright © 1974 by Lerner Publications Company.

Lothrop, Lee & Shepard Books, a division of William Morrow & Company, Inc.: Adapted text and illustrations from *Molly's Pilgrim* by Barbara Cohen, illustrated by Michael J. Deraney. Text copyright © 1983 by Barbara Cohen; illustratioons copyright © 1983 by Michael J. Deraney.

Macmillan Publishing Company: Adapted from *Away Goes Sally* by Elizabeth Coatsworth. Copyright 1934 by Macmillan Publishing Company; renewed 1962 by Elizabeth Coatsworth Beston. Adapted from *Galileo Galilei, Space Pioneer* (Titled: "Galileo") by Arthur S. Gregor, illustrated by James W. Williamson. Text copyright © 1965 by Arthur S. Gregor, illustrations copyright © 1965 by James W. Williamson. Adapted from pp. 18–42 in *Elisabeth, the Treasure Hunter* by Felice Holman, illustrated by Erik Blegvad. Text copyright © 1964 by Felice Holman; illustrations copyright © 1964 by Erik Blegvad.

McGraw-Hill Book Company: From pp. 91–92 and 116–117 in *Communities* by Leonard Martelli et al. Copyright © 1983 by McGraw-Hill, Inc. Published by McGraw-Hill Book Company.

William Morrow & Company, Inc.: Adapted from pp. 78–103 in "Ellen Rides Again" in *Ellen Tebbits* by Beverly Cleary. Copyright © 1951 by Beverly Cleary. "Beauty" from *I Am a Pueblo Indian Girl* by E-Yeh-Shure'. Copyright 1939 by William Morrow & Company, Inc.; renewed 1967 by Louise Abeita Chiwiwi.

Russell & Volkening, as agents for Harry Hartwick: Adapted from pp. 32–57 in *The Runaway Ride of Old 88* by Harry Hartwick. Copyright © 1971 by Harry Hartwick. Published by Little, Brown and Company.

Scholastic Inc.: Adapted from *Ty's One-man Band* by Mildred Pitts Walter. Copyright © 1980 by Mildred Pitts Walker.

Silver Burdett Company: From pp. 40–41, 45–47 in *Silver Burdett Science.* © 1984 by Silver Burdett Company.

Viking Penguin Inc.: Adapted from *Cam Jansen and the Mystery of the Television Dog* (Titled: "The Mystery of the Television Dog") by David Adler. Copyright © 1981 by David Adler. Illustrations from *Ox-Cart Man* by Donald Hall, illustrated by Barbara Cooney. Illustrations copyright © 1979 by Barbara Cooney Porter. Adapted from *Miss Rumphius,* story and pictures by Barbara Cooney. Copyright © 1982 by Barbara Cooney Porter.

Walker and Company: From *A First Look at Seashells* by Millicent E. Selsam and Joyce Hunt. Copyright © 1983 by Millicent E. Selsam and Joyce Hunt. Published by Walker and Company.

Albert Whitman & Company: Adapted from *My Dad Is Really Something* by Lois Osborn. Text © 1983 by Lois Osborn. Published by Albert Whitman & Company.

(continued on page 344)

Contents

Unit 3

Beauty

154

Unit 4 Milestones 232

Telescopes

Unit 1

Passports

A passport is a written paper that a traveler needs to enter another country. The word *passport* also can be used to mean a way of being accepted. For some people, learning can be a passport to being successful. An adventure can be a passport to change and to making new friends.

Each of the characters in this unit finds a passport to a change in his or her life. Would you like to travel to a new land where the way of living is very different from the way you live? What would you do to prove that you are old enough to do an important job?

Come aboard and travel with the characters in this unit. Don't forget your passport!

The shoemaker's passport is an unusual piece of leather. What adventures does the shoemaker have as he travels?

The Shoemaker's Gift

interpreted by Lyndell Ludwig

Many years ago, in a village in China, there lived a poor shoemaker. The shoemaker was skilled at making sandals and other footwear for the people in the village. One day the shoemaker found an unusual piece of leather. "What a fine piece of leather," he thought. "I will make a pair of hunting boots out of it."

The shoemaker worked hard on the boots. He worked in his spare time and often far into the quiet hours of the night.

When the boots were finished, his wife saw them and said, "What a handsome pair of boots! It would be a shame to sell them. You must take the boots and give them to the king."

The next day, the shoemaker started out toward the city where the king lived. The city was surrounded by a high wall. The shoemaker came to the main gate. When the guard who was watching at the gate saw the shoemaker, he blocked the shoemaker's way with his spear. "Halt!" said the guard to the shoemaker. "State your business or I cannot let you enter the city."

The shoemaker answered without a pause, "I have brought a present to give to the king."

The guard looked at the bundle the shoemaker was carrying. "When anyone gives the king a present and he accepts it," the guard said in a low voice, "the king always grants him something. If you will give me one-third of whatever the king gives you, I will let you go in." This did not seem right to the shoemaker, but he agreed, and the guard let him enter the city.

The shoemaker walked toward the palace. A second guard stood at the gate to the palace. When the shoemaker came to him, the guard stepped in front of him and blocked his way. "Halt!" he said. "State your business or you cannot enter the palace."

"I have a present to give the king," the shoemaker said.

The guard lowered his voice. "If you agree to give me one-third of whatever the king gives you, I will let you enter." Now the shoemaker thought that everyone in the city was a thief.

"All right, I will give you one-third of whatever the king gives me," he said. The second guard let the shoemaker enter the palace grounds.

The shoemaker walked toward the main hall. Just inside were two doors where a third guard watched. The guard stepped forward. "Halt!" he said. "State your business or I cannot let you in."

"I have come to give the king a present," the shoemaker said.

The guard lowered his voice to almost a whisper. "Not everyone can see the king," he said. "If you will promise to give me one-third of whatever the king gives you, I will let you go in."

The shoemaker answered without a pause. "I promise to give you one-third of whatever the king gives me." At once the third guard pulled open the doors.

The shoemaker knew that the three guards would take all of whatever the king might give him. Still, he entered the chambers of the king.

"Who are you?" asked the king.

"I am a village shoemaker. I made a pair of hunting boots and I have brought them here to give to you."

The king watched the shoemaker take out the hunting boots. Then the king tried the boots on and said, "I accept these boots. Now it is my turn to give you a gift."

The shoemaker said, "Would you, great king, order that one of your strongest guards give me ninety-nine blows with a hard wooden stick?"

"This is an unusual request," the king answered. He turned to his chief secretary and said, "I order that this shoemaker receive ninety-nine blows with a hard wooden stick."

The chief secretary led the shoemaker out of the king's chambers. The third guard was still on duty outside the two great doors. The shoemaker whispered to the guard, "Follow me, and I will see that you receive one-third of the king's gift."

At the palace entrance stood the second guard. The shoemaker bent toward him. "Follow me," he whispered. "I will see that you receive one-third of the king's gift."

When they reached the main gate to the city, the first guard stood watching outside. The shoemaker whispered, "Follow me, and I will see that you receive one-third of the gift the king has given me."

The little group walked a short distance and stopped outside the city gate. The shoemaker spoke. "Today I came to the city to give the king a present. I had to pass by these three guards. Each guard said he would let me pass only if I would agree to give him one-third of whatever the king gave me. I now request that the king's order be carried out. I request that one of the guards with a hard wooden stick strike each of the guards one-third of the ninety-nine blows."

The chief secretary spoke, "So this is how it is! By order of the king, each of you shall receive thirty-three blows."

A crowd was beginning to gather. "Long live the shoemaker! He has repaid those who tried to cheat him," they cried out.

The king heard the noise and sent a messenger to fetch the chief secretary. The secretary told him about how the three guards tried to cheat the shoemaker. The king ordered the shoemaker to be brought before him. When the shoemaker arrived the king said, "You did the right thing."

The shoemaker smiled and slowly backed away to leave. Since everyone leaving the king's presence had to keep his eyes lowered to the ground, the last thing the shoemaker saw of the king was the beautiful pair of hunting boots he had made with his own hands. The king was still wearing them.

1. What adventures did the shoemaker have because of the boots?

2. What lesson did the three guards learn?

3. How did the shoemaker pay the three guards part of his reward?

4. How did you feel when the chief secretary told the guards about their reward?

5. How did the author tell you that the king rewarded the shoemaker for the gift?

A hyphen (-) is used to write a compound word or to divide a word at the end of a line.

1. Below are four words as they appear in the story. Read the words and decide how the hyphen is used in each. Use the story if you need to.

   shoe-maker   one-third   mak-ing   ninety-nine

2. Find four compound words in the story that do not need a hyphen.

Prewrite

Think about the gift the shoemaker requested from the king. Read the last page of the selection again. Were the ninety-nine blows the only reward the shoemaker received? Explain your answer. What gift would you have asked for if you were the shoemaker? Why?

Compose

Choose one of the activities below.

1. Write a paragraph that tells about the real reward the shoemaker received. Do you think this reward was worth more than gold or silver? Explain your answer.

2. Pretend that you are the shoemaker. Write a paragraph that describes a gift you would ask the king to give you. Tell why you would ask for this gift.

Revise

Read your paragraph carefully. Make sure you have answered all the questions in the activity you have chosen. Make any changes that are needed.

Face to Face
by Anita E. Posey

I'd like to go around the world
    And get a chance to see
The boys and girls of other lands
    And let them all see me.

I'd like to meet them face to face,
    And get to know their names.
I'd like to sit and talk with them
    And learn to play their games.

I'd like to visit in their homes,
    Their family life to share.
I'd like to taste the food they eat,
    And see the clothes they wear.

I'd like to get to know them well
    Before my journey's end;
For only when you know someone
    Can he become your friend.

And so, someday, I'd like to go
    Around the world and see
The boys and girls of other lands
    And let them all see me.

Marco Polo is remembered for a journey he took a long time ago. What did he learn on this long journey? How did he share this information?

The Travels of Marco Polo

by Alma Marshak Whitney

Marco Polo lived in Venice, Italy, over seven hundred years ago. In the year 1271, Marco left Venice with his father and his uncle to go to China. Marco's father, Nicolò, and his uncle, Maffeo, had been to China before. They had become friendly with China's ruler, Kublai Khan, and they decided to return there.

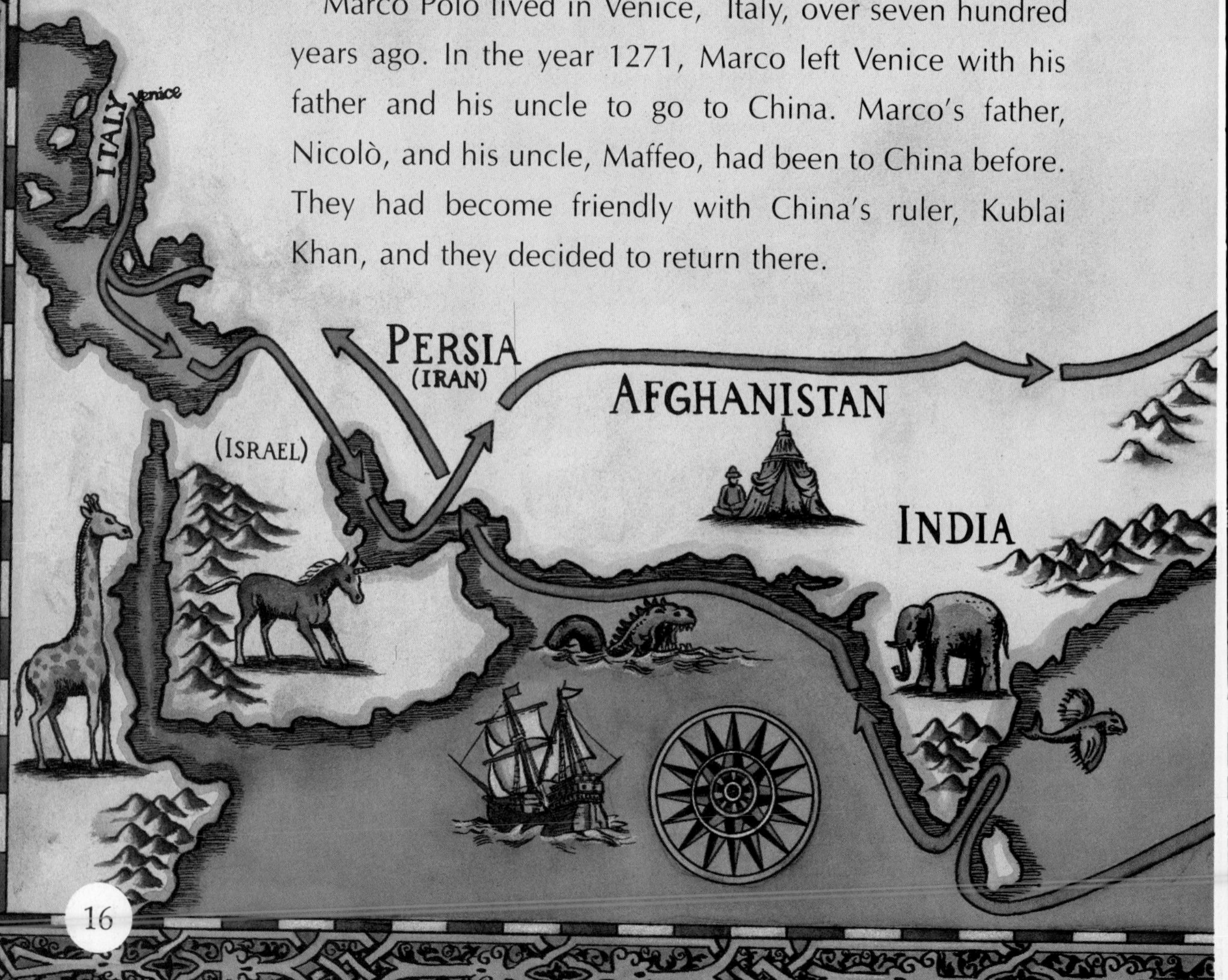

ITALY
Venice
(ISRAEL)
PERSIA (IRAN)
AFGHANISTAN
INDIA

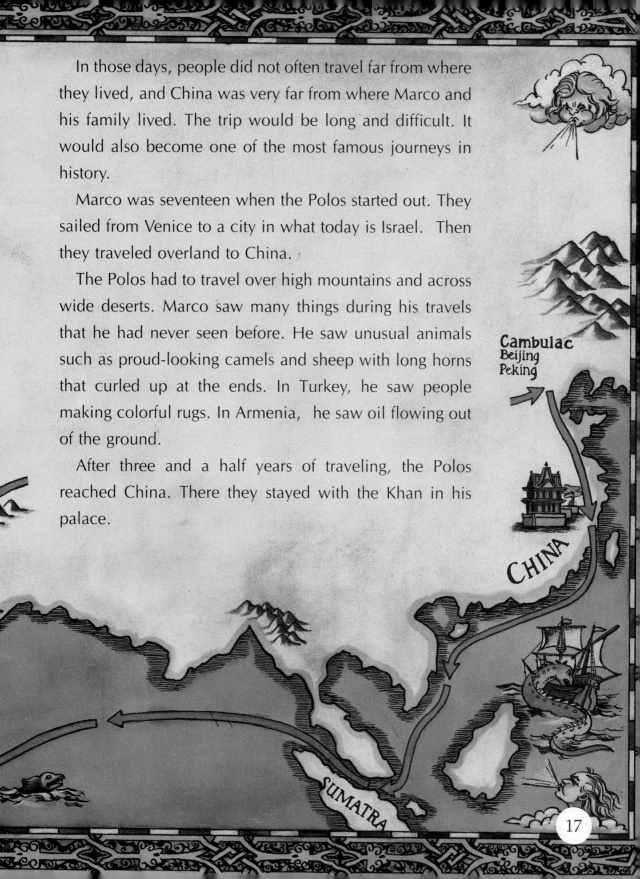

In those days, people did not often travel far from where they lived, and China was very far from where Marco and his family lived. The trip would be long and difficult. It would also become one of the most famous journeys in history.

Marco was seventeen when the Polos started out. They sailed from Venice to a city in what today is Israel. Then they traveled overland to China.

The Polos had to travel over high mountains and across wide deserts. Marco saw many things during his travels that he had never seen before. He saw unusual animals such as proud-looking camels and sheep with long horns that curled up at the ends. In Turkey, he saw people making colorful rugs. In Armenia, he saw oil flowing out of the ground.

After three and a half years of traveling, the Polos reached China. There they stayed with the Khan in his palace.

Cambulac
Beijing
Peking

CHINA

SUMATRA

In Peking, Marco discovered that people printed books by pressing paper on wooden blocks on which letters had been carved. In other parts of the world, books were still being copied by hand.

Marco soon learned four of the many languages spoken in China. Because Marco could speak four languages, the Khan asked him to travel throughout China as his "eyes and ears."

As Marco traveled through China, he saw things that were new to him. He saw narrow wooden roads built high up on the sides of steep mountains. In one place, a huge marble bridge spread across a wide river. Marco made notes that described what he saw so he would remember everything and be able to report back to the Khan.

After seventeen years in China, the Polos began their long journey home. The travelers sailed through rough seas. The first stop on their trip was Persia,[1] which today is Iran.[2] On the way to Persia, Marco took more notes.

[1] Persia [pûr'zhə]
[2] Iran [i•ran']

He wrote about spices growing in Java[1] and described strange animals such as rhinoceroses in Sumatra.[2] The trip to Persia took two years.

After the Polos left Persia, they traveled by land and sea back to Venice. The Polos had been away from Venice for twenty-four years. Marco was seventeen when he first left for China. Now, he was a man of forty-one.

Marco told many people about his travels. One of these people, a writer named Rustichello, said he thought the story of Marco's travels would make a good book. Marco and Rustichello worked together on the book. When it was finished, the book was called *A Description of the World*.

A Description of the World became very popular. Many people read the book. Some people did not believe the stories in it. They did not believe Marco had traveled as far or had seen the things he said he did.

Nearly two hundred years later, Christopher Columbus read the book and believed the stories of Marco's travels. When Columbus sailed from Spain, he took a copy of *A Description of the World* with him. While trying to find a way to sail to the places Marco Polo had described, Columbus landed in the New World.

---

[1] Java [jä′və]
[2] Sumatra [sōō•mä′trə]

1. Why was the story of Marco Polo's travels important to the people of Venice in 1295?

2. What new things did Marco Polo learn in China?

3. What makes you think that Marco Polo's stories were true?

4. Why was *A Description of the World* a good title for Marco Polo's book about his travels?

5. How did you know that people still thought about Marco Polo's adventures two hundred years after they happened?

Apply

the

Skills

Below are four events from Marco Polo's travels. Put the sentences in the correct time order.

a. Marco Polo arrived in China.

b. Marco Polo saw beautiful rugs in Turkey.

c. Marco Polo began his trip in 1271.

d. Marco Polo returned to Venice.

Prewrite

Marco Polo saw many things during his twenty-four-year trip. These things are described in his book. Some people did not believe the stories in Marco Polo's book. Why do you think this is so? What do you think would have been the most interesting thing Marco Polo saw during his travels?

Compose

Choose one of the activities below.

1. Write a paragraph that describes what you think would have been the most interesting thing Marco Polo did or saw during his travels. Tell why you think so.

2. Some people did not believe the stories in Marco Polo's book. Write a paragraph that tells two reasons why some people may not have believed the stories.

Revise

Check your work to make sure you have followed the directions in the activity.

21

Sequence

Look at the pictures below. Look for the order in which things happen.

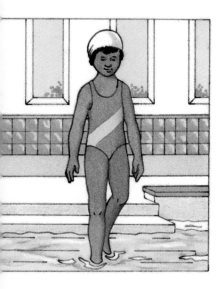  

These pictures show a time sequence. Before the girl can swim, she must first get into the water. Then she swims. When she is finished swimming, she gets out of the pool. This is called **time order.**

Recognizing time order is important in reading. Writers often tell about events in the order in which they happened. This helps the reader better understand what is being told.

Sometimes writers use clue words to show time order. A few of these words are *then, when, now, noon, today, later, before, until, after,* and *at first.* Dates are also time clues. Sometimes they are written as numerals: *1981.* Sometimes they are written as words: *Fourth of July, December,* and *Tuesday.*

As you read the paragraphs below, notice the dates the author used to help you follow the time order.

In October 1620, the *Mayflower* sailed from England. It was carrying about one hundred people who wanted a new start in America. The long trip took about two months. Finally, on December 21, 1620, the *Mayflower* landed in Plymouth, Massachusetts.

How long did the trip take? What dates were used to help you? The author used two different time clues. The dates October 1620 and December 21, 1620, should have helped you to see that the trip took two months. In addition, the author gave you more help with the words *about two months.*

at first

Tuesday   until   December

Fourth of July

1981

before   today   after   later   23

Textbook Application: Sequence in Social Studies

A social studies textbook can have many time clues. Read the following paragraphs. The sidenotes will help you find the time clues.

There are two time clues in this paragraph: *1865* and *then*. The date *1865* sets the time period. The word *then* shows what happened after 1865.

The date *1869* shows a time passage.

Instead of *1870*, the author wrote *One year later.*

The phrase *In the years that followed* shows more time passing.

The first railroad came to Kansas City in <u>1865</u>. <u>Then</u> the river town began to grow into a big city. The railroad brought more people. It connected Kansas City with cities in the East. It carried mail and supplies back and forth quickly.

In <u>1869</u>, the Hannibal Bridge was built. It was the first railroad bridge across the Missouri River. This meant that railroad trains could go farther west. <u>One year later</u>, eight different railroads connected Kansas City with other places.

<u>In the years that followed</u>, Kansas City became a marketplace for wheat. The wheat was grown on farms in the area. Railroads began bringing cattle from the West. Kansas City became a

center for the cattle trade. In 1885, the Kansas City stockyards were built. At this time, flour mills and meat-packing plants were started. These industries are still important to Kansas City.

—*Communities*, McGraw-Hill

1885 and the phrase *at this time* are two ways of showing the same time.

Read the next two paragraphs carefully to find the time order. No dates have been given.

For a long time, people walked wherever they went. Walking was their only means of transportation. Later, they may have ridden a horse. Or they might have ridden on a wagon pulled by a horse or other animal. They sent goods the same way. On water, they traveled in boats. They moved the boats with oars or sails.

Then, about 150 years ago, transportation began to change. Engines were used to move boats on water. They were used to pull loads on the ground. Because these engines were so heavy, they were put on iron tracks. This new means of transportation was called the railroad.

—*Communities*, McGraw-Hill

Time order helps you when you read. Dates tell when events happen. Other time clues also help.

Molly is learning many things about her new country. What do Molly and the other children learn about the Pilgrims from a homework assignment?

Molly's Pilgrim

by Barbara Cohen

Molly is a little Jewish girl who came with her family from Russia to live in the United States. Molly did not like going to school because her classmates made fun of the way she spoke. Elizabeth usually laughed the most and said mean things to Molly.

The students in Molly's third-grade class had been reading about Pilgrims and the first Thanksgiving. Molly had never heard of Thanksgiving and had trouble reading the word. Her teacher, Miss Stickley, told Molly to read the story and it would explain the meaning of Thanksgiving. As the story begins, Molly has just come home from school.

When I got home, Mama said to me, just like always, *"Nu, shaynkeit,* do you have any homework?"

"I need a clothespin," I said.

"A clothespin? What kind of homework is a clothespin?"

"I have to make a doll out of it. A Pilgrim doll."

Mama frowned. *"Nu, Malkeleh,* what's a Pilgrim?"

I searched for the words to explain "Pilgrim" to Mama. "Pilgrims came to this country from the other side," I said.

"Like us," Mama said.

That was true. "They came for religious freedom," I added. "They came so they could worship as they pleased."

Mama's eyes lit up. She seemed to understand. "Do you have any other homework?" she asked.

"Yes," I said. "I have ten arithmetic problems. They're hard."

"Do them," she said, "and then go out to play. I'll make the doll for you. I'll make it tonight. It'll be ready for you in the morning."

"Just make sure it's a girl doll," I said.

"Naturally," Mama replied. "Who ever heard of a boy doll?"

I didn't bother to explain.

The next morning, when I sat down at the table for breakfast, the doll was at my place. Maybe she had started out as a clothespin, but you'd never have known it to look at her. Mama had covered the clothespin with cloth and stuffing. She had made hair out of dark brown yarn and she'd embroidered eyes, a nose, and a mouth on the face. She had dressed the doll in a long, full red skirt, tiny black felt boots, and a bright yellow high-necked blouse. She had covered the yarn hair with a yellow kerchief embroidered with red flowers.

"She's gorgeous, Mama," I managed to murmur.

Mama smiled, satisfied.

"But Mama," I added slowly, "she doesn't look like the Pilgrim woman in the picture in my reading book."

"No?" Mama said.

"She looks like you in that photograph you have that was taken when you were a girl."

Mama's smile turned into a laugh. "Of course. I did that on purpose."

"You did, Mama? Why?"

"What's a Pilgrim, *shaynkeit*?" Mama asked. "A Pilgrim is someone who came here from the other side to find freedom. That's me, Molly. I'm a Pilgrim!"

I was sure there was something wrong with what Mama was saying. She was not the kind of Pilgrim Miss Stickley or the reading book had been talking about. But it was too late to make another doll now. All I could do was take the only one I had to school with me.

Most of the dolls were out on the desks. I had carried mine in a little paper bag. I put it inside my desk without even taking it out of the bag.

The bell hadn't rung yet. Elizabeth and Hilda were walking up and down the aisles, pointing to the dolls and whispering. When they came to my desk, Elizabeth said in a low voice, "Miss Stickley's going to be mad at you, jolly Molly. She doesn't like people who don't do their homework."

"I did it," I muttered.

"Well, then, let's see it."

I shook my head.

"You didn't do it," Elizabeth taunted. "You didn't, you didn't."

I opened the desk and took out the paper bag. I closed the desk and set the bag on top. Slowly, I pulled out the doll.

"Oh, my goodness," Elizabeth sighed. "How can anyone be as dumb as you, jolly Molly? That's not a Pilgrim. Miss Stickley is going to be really mad at you. Miss

Stickley's going to get you this time."

My face felt hot as fire. I looked down at my desk top.

The bell rang. Elizabeth and Hilda rushed to their seats. I shoved the doll back into my desk.

After morning exercises, Miss Stickley began to walk around the room, just as Elizabeth had. She looked at each one of the dolls. "Why Michael, what a magnificent headdress. Where did you find so many feathers? . . . Sally, she's lovely. Such an interesting face. . . . Such beautiful gray silk, Elizabeth. Yours is a very rich Pilgrim."

"I think she's the best so far," Elizabeth said.

"Well, she's very good," Miss Stickley allowed.

Then Miss Stickley came to me. Without looking up, I pulled my doll out of the desk.

I heard Elizabeth laugh out loud. "My goodness, Molly," she cried. "That's not a Pilgrim. That's some Russian or Polish person. What does a person like that have to do with Pilgrims?"

"She's very beautiful," Miss Stickley said. "Perhaps Molly just didn't understand."

I looked up at Miss Stickley. "Mama said . . ." I began.

Elizabeth giggled again.

Miss Stickley put her hand on my shoulder. "Tell me what your Mama said, Molly."

"This doll is dressed like Mama," I explained slowly. "Mama came to America for religious freedom, too. Mama said she's a Pilgrim."

Elizabeth hooted. She wasn't the only one.

Miss Stickley marched up to the front of the room. She turned and faced the class. "Listen to me, Elizabeth," she said in a loud voice. "Listen to me, all of you. Molly's mother *is* a Pilgrim. She's a modern Pilgrim. She came here, just like the Pilgrims long ago, so she could worship in her own way, in peace and freedom." Miss Stickley stared at Elizabeth. "Elizabeth, do you know where the Pilgrims got the idea for Thanksgiving?"

"They just thought it up, Miss Stickley," Elizabeth said.

"No, Elizabeth," Miss Stickley replied. "They knew about the Jewish harvest holiday."

I knew that holiday, too. We called it Sukkos.

"The Pilgrims got the idea for Thanksgiving from Jews like Molly and her mama." Miss Stickley marched down the aisle to my desk again. "May I have your doll for a while, Molly?"

"Sure," I said.

"I'm going to put this beautiful doll on my desk," Miss Stickley announced, "where everyone can see it all the time. It will remind us all that Pilgrims are still coming to

America." She smiled at me. "I'd like to meet your mama, Molly. Please ask her to come to see me one day after school."

"Your doll is the most beautiful, Molly," Emma said. Emma sat next to me. "Your doll is the most beautiful one of all."

I nodded. "Yes," I said. "I know."

I decided if Miss Stickley actually invited her, it was all right for Mama to come to school. I decided something else, too. I decided it takes all kinds of Pilgrims to make a Thanksgiving.

1. What did Molly and the other children learn about Pilgrims?

2. Why did Miss Stickley put Molly's clothespin doll on her desk?

3. What did Molly understand about Thanksgiving at the end of the story?

4. How did you feel when Elizabeth laughed at Molly?

5. How did you know that Molly's mother understood the meaning of being a Pilgrim?

Read the following sentences. Find the words in the sentences that the author uses to tell when something happens.

1. The next morning when I sat down at the table for breakfast, the doll was at my place.

2. After morning exercises, Miss Stickley began to walk around the room . . .

3. Then Miss Stickley came to me.

Prewrite

In "Molly's Pilgrim" the author uses time order clues to let the reader know when things happen. The list below gives some examples of clue words.

when	then	tonight
now	after	morning

Compose

Choose one of the activities below.

1. Write a paragraph that describes your day at school. Use time order clues like the ones listed above to tell when things happen.

2. Use time order clues to write a descriptive paragraph about a trip you have taken. It may be a make-believe or a real story. Give dates, times, and other clues to let the readers know when things happened.

Revise

Read your work carefully. Did you use enough time order clues so that the readers will know the order in which things happen? If not, add more time order clues to your paragraph.

Diagrams

A **diagram** is a drawing used to explain how something is put together or how it works. Diagrams often have labels on them. **Labels** are words that show the important parts of the diagram. Sometimes lines connect the labels to parts of the diagram. Sometimes a diagram has a caption. The **caption** gives additional information about the diagram.

Look at the diagram of the sailboat below. What parts of the sailboat have labels? Now look at the caption below the diagram. What does the caption tell about a sailboat?

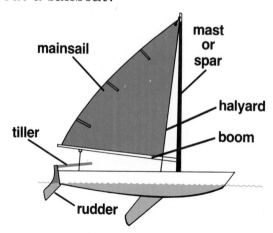

The mainsail is attached to the mast by a rope called the halyard. When the mainsail catches the wind, the sailboat moves.

Read the paragraph below. As you are reading, look at the diagram and the labeled parts.

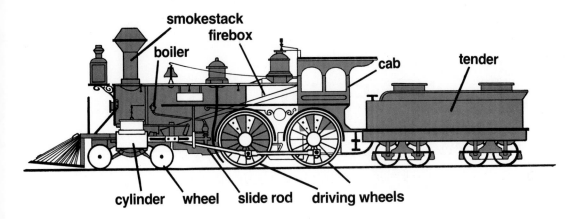

A steam-engine locomotive has a boiler. Coal is burned in the firebox to heat water in the boiler. This heated water makes steam. The steam goes from the boiler into the cylinders. In each cylinder is a piston. Steam makes the pistons move, and the pistons make the wheels of the locomotive move. From the pistons, the steam goes through the smokestack and out of the engine, making the "choo-choo" sound of the steam-engine locomotive.

The diagram and labels should have helped you understand how a steam engine works. A diagram is useful for understanding how things work or how things are put together.

Steam-engine locomotives were often used to transport people and freight. Find out how a steam engine works. Use the diagram to help you.

Steam-engine Freight Trains

by Marsha Newfield

Long ago, trains were pulled by steam-engine locomotives. A trip on a train started out in the freight yard. The freight was put into each railroad car. The locomotive was added to the string of railroad cars to pull the train.

The steam engine was in the locomotive. A steam engine burned coal to heat water. A car, or tender, filled with coal and water was right behind the locomotive. A fire was built in the firebox. The fire heated water in a boiler and steam was formed. The steam pushed the parts connected to the wheels and that made the locomotive move.

The engineer and the fireman rode in the cab of the locomotive. The engineer ran the train. The fireman's job was to keep the fire burning in the firebox. This was done by throwing coal into the firebox. The engineer and the fireman also kept their eyes on the track ahead. They watched for cows and other trains. It wasn't always easy to see out of the cab window because smoke and steam rose out of the smokestack in front of the cab.

The engineer used a wooden hand brake to stop the train. The whole train could not be stopped at once. Each car had its own hand brake, which was on top of the car. The engineer had to signal the other crew members in order to bring the whole train to a stop. He signaled them by pulling the cord of the train whistle. The crew members then would climb up on the top of each car and turn the hand brake. Turning the hand brakes took a long time. After air brakes were invented, all the cars could be stopped at once. The crew used the hand brakes only if the air brakes did not work.

The last car on the train was called the caboose. It was also where the crew lived on long trips. It had beds, chairs, and a place to cook. Many cabooses were painted red. Many cabooses had high towers so that the crew could look out to see what was ahead.

The train whistle was very important. Different whistle sounds meant different things. Each sound was part of a code. One short whistle meant to stop the train. One long whistle meant the train was coming to a station.

There was also a whistle signal for backing off the main track onto a small side track called a siding. Since there was only one set of tracks, one train had to wait on the siding while the other train rode on the main track.

There was a telegraph machine and an agent at each station. Telegraph messages helped tell the crew what was ahead. The engineer had to know about any possible trouble on the tracks so he could begin to change plans.

The train received a telegraph message from a station agent. The train slowed down at the station, but did not stop. The station agent either threw the message to the fireman on the moving train, or the agent put the message on the end of a long pole and held it out for the fireman to grab.

The trip ended at the freight yard. The same cars might stay together for the return trip home or new cars might be added. Then the train was loaded again with freight, and the return trip was begun.

Discuss the Selection

1. Why does a steam-engine locomotive need a fireman?

2. Why did the trip start and end in a freight yard?

3. How was the whistle important?

4. Which crew member do you think had the hardest job?

5. How do you know that the train crew no longer stops the train with hand brakes?

Apply the Skills

A diagram shows how something works.

1. On a sheet of paper, draw a picture of a train. Label the locomotive, the tender, the freight car, and the caboose. Draw a line from each label to the correct part.

2. In which car would each of the following things be found?

   a. steam engine

   b. coal and water

Prewrite

A diagram and caption were used to help describe a steam-engine freight train. Think about how you would describe a certain car, house, or plant to someone. How would a diagram and caption help someone understand your description?

Compose

Draw a diagram. It can be a diagram of a car, a plant, or anything else you choose. Label each part of the diagram. Then write a caption that describes the diagram. Use two or three sentences for the caption.

Revise

Did you remember to label each part of the diagram? Does your caption describe the diagram you drew? If not, revise your work.

A train ride turns into a dangerous and exciting adventure. What events take place on this ride?

The Runaway Ride of Old 88

by Harry Hartwick

Very carefully, Dave, the engineer, headed the freight train down the mountain. Then he let out the air brakes so the train could pick up a little speed. When the train had reached a faster speed, Dave tested the air brakes again. The brakes, which had been perfect only a moment ago, no longer worked! The train was starting to go faster.

Again he tried the brakes, but they still did not work. The train was gaining speed all the time. "No brakes!" Dave yelled. He signaled the brakemen and conductor to climb on top of the swaying cars and set the hand brakes.

As it went around the first curve, the train tried to leave the tracks—but held on. Looking back, Dave could see the conductor and two brakemen climb from the caboose onto the top of the cars. They ran along the catwalk trying to keep from being thrown off the moving cars.

When all the hand brakes had been tightened, Dave tested the air brakes again. Still the brakes were not working. Engine No. 88 was running free. There was no way to stop it. The train would just have to run till it reached the bottom of the mountain where the track leveled off or till it met something that stopped it. That something would probably be the night passenger train, No. 64.

Dave's orders called for No. 88 to head off onto a siding at Hamlin Crossing and let No. 64 go through. At this rate No. 88 would never be able to turn off the main line. The two trains could crash head-on unless they could get word to No. 64 before it reached Parkersville. To do this Dave would have to get a message to the station agent at Cantwell. Then the agent could send a message to Parkersville in time to get No. 64 off the main track.

The train gained speed as it ran down the track into Cantwell. Dave yelled to Spike, "Write a note— we'll throw it off—tell the agent to hold No. 64 at Parkersville!"

Spike nodded. He wrote a few words on a scrap of paper and wrapped it around a piece of coal.

As the train flew past the station, the agent stood on the platform. His mouth hung open in surprise.

Dave took the coal from Spike and held it up so the station agent could see it. Then he threw it very hard toward the station. The coal hit the ground and came apart. The paper blew along the platform where the station agent trapped it and picked it up. Dave could see the agent anxiously reading the note, and then running for the telegraph office door.

Telegraph poles were flying past the cab window in a steady blur. The wheels of the great train were pounding over the track. Dust was dancing on the floor of the swaying cab as the train flew through Hamlin Crossing, the place where they were to go onto a siding until No. 64 passed.

The wind beat at Dave's face as he anxiously stared at the track ahead. This curve was it! It led to Parkersville. If their note had worked, the track would be clear. If it hadn't, No. 64 would be coming right at them.

If they found No. 64 staring them in the face when the train rounded the bend, the crew would have to jump from the cab, and hope to save their lives that way. Dave called Spike to his side, and yelled to him, "Get ready to jump! Don't go till I tell you!"

Dave wanted to close his eyes as the train swept around the bend. He had to make himself look. Any moment he expected the crash to take place. He could see Spike standing just above the steps on his side of the cab, ready to jump. He got ready to jump himself.

As the train sped around the curve, Dave gave a happy cry. The track was clear! Far ahead, beyond the Parkersville station, he could see passenger train No. 64 sitting safely on the siding. A few seconds later, No. 88 roared past the passenger train.

Freight train No. 88 began to slow down as the track leveled off and began to climb into the mountains on the other side of Parkersville. Finally, three miles beyond the town, No. 88 stopped. It began to roll backward down toward the station. It passed the station, as a great cheer went up from the crowd that had gathered there. Then it rolled to a complete stop.

Dave turned and threw his arms around Spike, and for a moment they slapped each other on the back, shaking and laughing at the same time.

"They'll never get me on that engine again!" cried Spike, shaking his head.

They never did. Two weeks later Engine No. 88 was retired and put on a stretch of lonely track on the outside of the yards. There it sits to this day with its wheels rusted to the tracks and its bell hanging quietly.

1. What are two reasons the train ride was a dangerous adventure?

2. What problem did the brakes cause when they no longer worked?

3. Why did the train slow down and finally stop?

4. Did you agree with Spike when he said, "They'll never get me on that engine again!" Why?

5. When did you know that there would not be a crash?

The sequence in a story, the order in which things happen, is important. Dave, the engineer, did things in a sequence.

1. First, Dave let out the air brakes. What did Dave do next?

2. What did Dave do before the train went around the curve that led to Parkersville?

Prewrite

"The Runaway Ride of Old 88" and "Steam-engine Freight Trains" are both about freight trains. In what ways are the selections different? Which selection did you think was more interesting? Why?

Compose

Choose one of the activities below.

1. Write a paragraph that tells how the two selections about trains are different. You should be able to write about at least two differences between the two selections.

2. Write a paragraph that tells which of the two selections about trains you enjoyed more. Explain why you liked one selection better than the other.

Revise

Read your paragraph to see if there are changes you should make in your work. Remember, both activities asked you to write about differences.

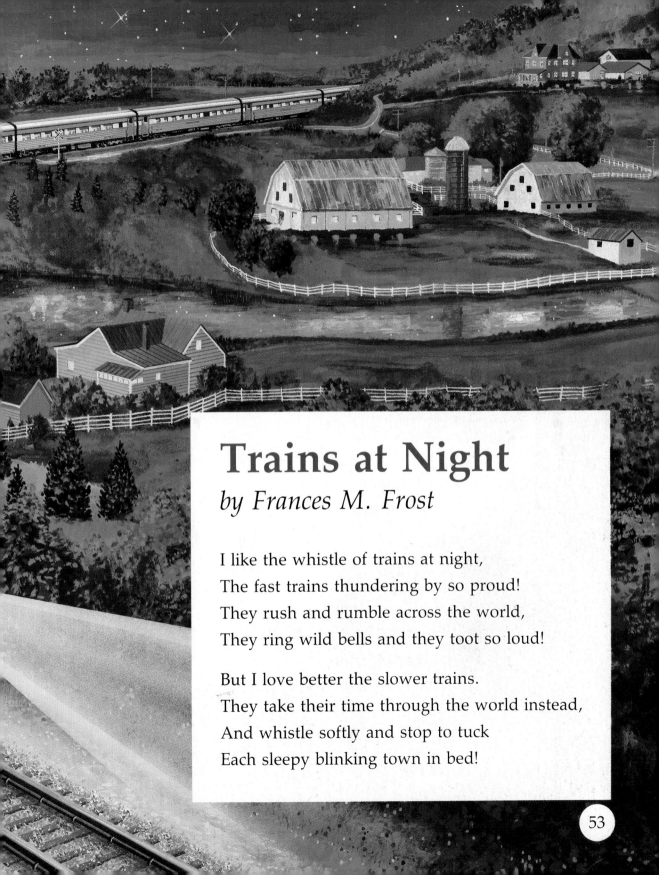

Trains at Night
by Frances M. Frost

I like the whistle of trains at night,
The fast trains thundering by so proud!
They rush and rumble across the world,
They ring wild bells and they toot so loud!

But I love better the slower trains.
They take their time through the world instead,
And whistle softly and stop to tuck
Each sleepy blinking town in bed!

53

Characterization

An author uses several ways to help you understand characters in stories. Read the paragraph below to see one way an author does this.

Evelyn was a very happy girl. Her parents had promised her that she could have a birthday party next week. They told her she could invite ten friends to the party.

In this paragraph, you learn that the character Evelyn is a happy girl, and why she is happy. The author states this information.

Now read the next paragraph to discover another way in which an author might help you understand the same character.

"Happy birthday to me, happy birthday to me," Evelyn sang as she raked a corner of the yard. "I just can't wait until next week," she thought. "I'm so happy. I hope my friends come to the party."

In the paragraph you just read, the author is telling what the character Evelyn is doing and thinking. From Evelyn's words, thoughts, and actions, you learn how she feels and why she feels that way.

Now read to discover still another way in which an author might help you understand Evelyn.

Mr. and Mrs. Vernon stood at the dining room window, watching their daughter Evelyn as she raked the leaves in the backyard.

"Have you ever seen Evelyn quite so happy?" Mr. Vernon asked. "I think our promising her a party for her birthday was a very good idea."

"I agree," replied Mrs. Vernon, "and I think our letting her invite ten friends is making her especially happy."

In these paragraphs, the author helps us understand the character Evelyn by what other characters in the story say about her.

As you read, look for some of the ways in which an author helps us understand a character.
The author may:
• describe the character;
• tell what the character thinks, says, and does;
• use other characters to tell about a character.

How is the truth the passport to changes in Tracy? How does the author help you see these changes?

The Girl Who Knew It All

by Patricia Reilly Giff

At the beginning of the summer, Tracy brought home a note from school that said she must read every day. Somehow Tracy never found the time to do this.

When Tracy saw that the shutters on an empty house down the street had been poorly painted, she tried to fix them. She misread the label on the can, and put red paint on the shutters instead of turpentine. Tracy didn't know that the new principal, Mrs. Bemus, was moving into the house.

As this story begins, Mrs. Bemus and Tracy are friends. Mrs. Bemus is taking Tracy and her sick dog to the vet.

The trip to the vet seemed to take forever. Finally Mrs. Bemus stopped in front of Dr. Wayne's office.

Tracy carried her quivering dog, Rebel, into the office.

Mrs. Wayne was in the reception room and said, "Take him right back into the doctor's office."

Dr. Wayne looked over his glasses at Tracy as she laid Rebel on the table. "I see you're still not watching what this dog eats," he said as he shook his head.

Dr. Wayne was touching Rebel carefully and looking in his eyes and ears and listening to his heart.

Finally he looked up and asked, "What have you fed this dog lately?"

"Let's see." Tracy tried to remember. "We had cereal this morning. For supper last night my mother gave him dog food." For a minute she almost decided not to tell what she and Rebel had eaten for a snack last night, but then she sighed and blurted out the rest of the list. "Two pieces of pizza, one each, a bowl of popcorn, half a . . ."

"Enough," Dr. Wayne said. "An upset stomach. It's a wonder you don't have one, too. I'm going to give Rebel some medicine now to make his stomach feel better. Take the rest home and give it to him three times a day."

Tracy placed her hands under Rebel's quivering body and took the medicine from Dr. Wayne as she backed out of the room.

Mrs. Bemus was waiting in the reception room. "Is it anything serious?" she asked.

"He has an upset stomach," Tracy answered.

On the way home Mrs. Bemus asked, "What are your friends doing on such a beautiful day?"

Tracy had almost forgotten. "Everyone is trying to get money for the fair. They're putting on a play," she said. Tracy tried to think of something else to talk about. Finally she cleared her throat and said, "Thank you for taking me to Dr. Wayne. I was really worried about Rebel."

"Glad to do it, Tracy, since you've been such a help to me."

She glanced at Mrs. Bemus to see if she was serious. "I've been a help?"

"I found fish for my cat on the back porch three times this week," Mrs. Bemus replied.

"I owed you," Tracy said without thinking.

For several seconds they did not speak. By now Mrs. Bemus was driving up High Flats Road. "I'm the one who painted your house," Tracy blurted out. "My reading's a mess, too."

Mrs. Bemus stopped the car in front of Tracy's house. She looked at Tracy seriously. "Why don't you put Rebel inside, and then come down to my house and we'll talk about it," she said.

Tracy lifted Rebel out of the car and closed the door with her hip. Inside, she laid Rebel gently on the living room rug. "You'll be all right," she said. "I have to see Mrs. Bemus, but I'll be back soon."

Before Tracy could even ring the bell, the screen door swung open. "Come on into the kitchen," Mrs. Bemus said. "Let's talk."

In the kitchen Tracy began, "I didn't mean . . . I couldn't read the label . . . I mean, I just wanted to fix the house up. Smooth it out with turpentine. I thought it was turpentine, but the paint can said *Turkey Red.*" Tracy glanced at Mrs. Bemus. Mrs. Bemus seemed to be staring at the floor.

Tracy began again. "All because I can't read. If I didn't have to read, everything would be perfect," she sighed. "Casey isn't going to be my friend any-more, and Leroy thinks I'm dumb. I'm not even going to be in the play, and it was all my idea . . ." her voice trailed off.

"All this happened because you're having trouble with reading?" Mrs. Bemus asked.

Tracy nodded, "It makes me get into all kinds of messes."

"Is that why you and Casey aren't friends anymore?"

"Well," she said, "Casey did say she'd help me with the reading."

"When is she going to start?"

Tracy lowered her head, "I told her I didn't want her help."

"All this because you're having trouble with reading," Mrs. Bemus said again.

"I . . ." Tracy said and stopped. Somehow that seemed backward. She was blaming all her problems on reading, but the truth was she was too lazy to practice her reading. She tried to make up for it by acting as if she knew everything in the whole round world.

Tracy took a deep breath and said, "I'm really sorry about your house. I was going to earn about a hundred dollars with the play and give you a whole bunch of money to get the house painted again."

Mrs. Bemus said, "You know, Tracy, I'm getting used to the house. No one else around here has red cabbages painted on the shutters."

"Cabbages! They were supposed to be roses," Tracy said.

Mrs. Bemus said, "Yes. I can see that now. I think I'll keep them. I didn't have the garage painted with the house. If you and some of those friends of yours want to make some money for the fair, I'd like to have you do it for me."

"Do you mean it? You could just pay the rest of the kids. It will make up for the first mess."

"That seems fair," Mrs. Bemus said. "Let me know when you're ready to begin."

After lunch, Tracy walked to Leroy's house.

"Want to help paint Mrs. Bemus's garage for money?"

Leroy said, "I suppose you'll be the boss."

"I don't have to be the boss," Tracy answered.

"All right," Leroy said. "Sure, I'll do it."

"How about getting Richard?" Tracy said. "We need all the hands we can get. Then meet me at Mrs. Bemus's garage and wait for me. I have to go see Casey."

She walked to Casey's house. "Casey!" she shouted.

Casey popped her head out of a window.

"Casey," she said again. "How would you like me to teach you how to paint a garage?"

Casey smiled back. "How would you like me to teach you how to read?"

"I'd like you to help me. I really would," Tracy replied.

Casey came down the steps. Tracy grabbed her hand, and together they ran toward the principal's house.

1. What problems did Tracy have when she didn't face the truth?

2. Why did Tracy's friends accept her again?

3. How did Mrs. Bemus help solve Tracy's problem?

4. How did you feel when Tracy was explaining her problems to Mrs. Bemus?

5. When did you know that Tracy would tell Mrs. Bemus the truth?

Below are several of Tracy's characteristics. Find a sentence from the story that explains each characteristic. The first one has been done for you.

1. *was trying to change the way she acted.* "I don't have to be the boss," Tracy answered.

2. *wasn't a very good reader*

3. *was sorry when she made mistakes*

Prewrite

The author of "The Girl Who Knew It All" described the main character, Tracy, to help the reader understand the character. Think about Tracy. If you were Mrs. Bemus, the principal, how would you describe Tracy? If you were Tracy, how would you describe yourself?

Compose

Choose one of the activities below.

1. Pretend that you are Mrs. Bemus. Write a description of Tracy. Tell about Tracy and how you think Tracy feels about herself.

2. Write a description of Tracy as if you were Tracy. Include details that would help the reader understand who you are, what you look like, and what you like and don't like.

Revise

Is the paragraph you have written a good description of Tracy as she sees herself or as Mrs. Bemus sees her? Do you need to add more details? Make any changes that are needed.

How does Matuk's adventure show his father that Matuk is growing up? As you read, look for details that show what Matuk is like.

Matuk, the Eskimo Boy

by Vee Cawston

Carrying the spear he had just made and an empty bag, Matuk went with the puppies, Kunik and Tupak, through the snow. The young dogs raced, tumbling and nipping each other's heels. Suddenly, Matuk saw two black objects moving far out on the sea ice. They disappeared so quickly it was hard to believe he had really seen anything. He was sure that two seals had just dived back into the clear, deep water.

What should he do? Matuk thought of how proud he would be to tell such good news in the village. Yet, if he ran back to get a harpoon, he might not be able to find the place again. He decided that a good hunter would first put up a marker. Matuk caught up his spear and the empty bag and hurried across the slippery stones to the ridges of ice along the shore. Kunik and Tupak followed at his heels as he ran toward the spot where he had seen the seals disappear.

Soon Matuk came to a wide crack in the ice. When he peered over the edge, he could see that the ice sloped downward to the water far below. It would be easy for seals to climb up here to sun themselves. "I think this is the place," Matuk said to his dogs. He walked on a few steps and saw the marks where the seals had been resting. If nothing frightened them, they would come back.

Matuk shoved his spear upright into a crack in the ice for the marker and hung the sealskin bag on it. Then he sat down for a moment, pulling Kunik and Tupak close to his side to keep them quiet. Matuk waited, listening and hoping that a seal would bark. The little dogs began to wiggle and nip at each other. Matuk clung to them tightly, and they didn't like that a bit. Suddenly, Tupak got away and ran along the edge, making fierce little growls at nothing.

"Come back, Tupak! Keep quiet!" shouted Matuk, but the puppy paid no attention. Matuk tried to catch him. Both dogs, however, seemed to think it was a game. They barked and bounced and raced around as though it were great fun!

Then a terrible thing happened. Tupak jumped back too far and disappeared. Matuk ran to the edge of the ice and looked down. There was Tupak just out of reach, digging his toenails into the rough ice and crying with fright. He might slip farther at any moment.

Matuk shouted loudly for help. He could still see the village, but it was too far away. He didn't feel grown up now. He had to do something. He looked back at his spear and knew that Tupak couldn't hold on to that. "But I can!" he cried and ran to fetch it.

At the spot where Tupak had fallen over, Matuk drove the spear into the ice with all his strength. He lowered himself, feet first, over the edge of the hole. Kunik came as close as she dared to watch them, and whined softly.

With his free arm, Matuk could just reach Tupak. He grabbed him. Very slowly, Matuk lifted the frightened puppy a little closer to him. Soon he had his arm around Tupak. Matuk stood on a shelf in the sloping ice. He shoved Tupak up over the edge to safety.

Matuk could now reach his spear with both hands. How tired his arms were! He began to wonder if he had enough strength to pull himself out.

At that moment, both dogs began to bark at something that Matuk could not see. Off they ran, barking at their discovery.

Matuk knew he must get out of the hole quickly before Kunik and Tupak got into more trouble. Stretching, he pulled himself up on his elbows.

All at once he heard a shout, and he could see his father running toward him.

His father lifted Matuk out of the hole. He lay stomach-down on the ice, too tired to open his eyes or speak.

When Matuk could move again, he saw that his father had pulled out the spear and was peering at it carefully. "It is strong and well-made," he said, as if surprised. "What were you doing with this?"

Matuk sat up slowly. "I marked the seal's hole for you."

"Did you fall into it?" continued his father.

"No . . . Tupak did," answered Matuk. He knew it would be better to explain everything.

When Matuk's father had heard the story, he said, "You remembered that a hunter thinks of others first and does his best when there is any danger." He looked down at Kunik and Tupak. "They are small and foolish yet. Take them home. Then come back and you and I will wait for these seals together."

Matuk did not need to be told twice. "There will be a big feast in the village today," Matuk said proudly.

1. What detail does the author include that helps Matuk's father see that Matuk is growing up?

2. How did Matuk's father reward Matuk for his bravery?

3. Why did Matuk need to be rescued?

4. Why do you think finding the seals would be good news for Matuk's village?

5. When did you first know that Matuk's father knew Matuk was growing up?

In this story, details show that Matuk is a very smart boy and a good hunter. Find the sentences below that tell this.

1. Soon Matuk came to a wide crack in the ice.

2. He decided that a good hunter would first put up a marker.

3. Matuk knew he must get out of the hole quickly.

Prewrite

Matuk, the boy in the story, may be very different from you. How did Matuk show he was growing up? How is Matuk's life different from your life?

Compose

Choose one of the activities below.

1. Write a paragraph that tells three things Matuk did that showed his father he was growing up. Reread the story if you have trouble remembering it. Tell how Matuk's father showed that he was proud of Matuk.

2. Pretend that you have just spent a day with Matuk. Write a paragraph that describes three ways in which Matuk's life might be different from your own.

Revise

Make sure you have stated the main idea of your paragraph. You should have supported your main idea with at least three details. Make changes if they are needed.

Thinking About "Passports"

Your journey through "Passports" is ended, but the adventures you read about may stay with you for a long time. Think about how a gift helped the shoemaker teach a lesson. Remember how Molly learned to be proud of her background. Think about what Tracy learned about herself that helped her solve her problems.

How did the author of each story help you get to know the characters better? Was it through the way the characters were described? Was it by what the characters said and did? Or was it by the characters' thoughts and feelings?

Each of the characters you read about in this unit used some type of passport to learn something, to grow as a person, and to become happier. You may discover that characters in other stories you read are looking for some of these things. As you read, decide how a character is moving toward a change. Ask yourself what that character's passport is.

1. The theme of "Passports" is that changes help people grow. How did the main characters in "The Girl Who Knew It All" and "Matuk, the Eskimo Boy" grow through a change?

2. What problem did each main character in a fiction selection in this unit have to solve?

3. Which characters had to solve a problem and think quickly when something new happened?

4. Which characters faced things that helped them learn about new ideas?

5. Which character wanted to tell people about unbelievable things?

Read on Your Own

Shadow Bear by Jim Arnosky. Doubleday. When
George, an Eskimo boy, meets Tarrak, a polar bear
cub, they are both in for a surprise.

Trains by Ray Broekel. Childrens Press. This book
tells about different kinds of trains, train workers,
and train stations.

The Carp in the Bathtub by Barbara Cohen. Lothrop.
Two children befriend and save a fish that their
mother intends to cook for a very special holiday
dinner.

The Adventures of Marco Polo by Demi. Holt. This is a
biography of the thirteenth-century explorer who
spent seventeen years in Asia and became a friend
of the emperor of China.

Yesterday's Trains by Patrick C. Dorin. Lerner. This
book tells the history of trains from steam engines
to diesel locomotives. It also tells what an overnight trip on a Pullman sleeper was like in the
1930's.

The Girl Who Knew It All by Patricia Reilly Giff. Delacorte. This is a story about a girl who blames all her problems on reading. A part of this book appears in this unit.

The Train by David McPhail. Little, Brown. During the night, when everyone is asleep, a boy takes an imaginary ride on his toy train.

Alina: A Russian Girl Comes to Israel by Mira Meir. Jewish Publication. This is the story of a girl who moves from Russia to Israel. She feels out of place in her new country.

The Railroad Book by E. Boyd Smith. Houghton. Two children learn about trains when the railroad opens up a line behind their garden fence.

Pettranella by Betty Waterton. Vanguard. Pettranella's family takes a long journey from a far-off country to Wisconsin. Her grandmother, who cannot make the long journey, gives her some seeds to plant at her new home.

Unit 2

Portholes

A porthole is a small opening or window in the side of a ship. If two people look through the same porthole, they may see two different things, or they may see the same thing differently.

Looking into a mirror also can be like looking through a porthole. You may not see yourself the way others see you.

When you read the stories in this unit, pretend you are looking at the characters through a porthole. Watch closely. Does the way they see things change? What do they do because of the changes? You may want to ask yourself what you would do if the same things happened to you. As you read, see if your view of the characters changes.

Miss Moody likes to walk on the beach after a storm. What does she find on the beach that could cause her a problem? How does she solve the problem?

Do Not Open

story and pictures by Brinton Turkle

Miss Moody lived at land's end with Captain Kidd. Captain Kidd wasn't the famous pirate; he was a cat. One morning after a storm, Miss Moody found him washed up on the beach. He was nearly drowned. She took care of him until he was well, and he repaid her kindness by keeping her cottage free of mice.

Captain Kidd hated storms. Miss Moody loved them. Just about everything in her cottage had been found on the beach after a storm, even the handsome banjo clock over her fireplace. The only thing wrong with the clock was that it wouldn't go. The hands always pointed to twenty minutes to four o'clock.

Late one September afternoon, the sky grew dark. A strong wind started to blow. Miss Moody knew what was coming. She shut the windows and lit a cheery fire in the fireplace. Captain Kidd wouldn't come out from under the bed.

Lightning flashed. Thunder crashed. Rain dashed against the windows.

Was Miss Moody worried? Not a bit. Her sturdy house had been built by a sea captain. It could ride out any storm. She smiled as she wondered what surprises might be on the beach in the morning.

After a quick breakfast the next morning, Miss Moody got out the old wheelbarrow. She and Captain Kidd were ready for the treasure hunt.

The first thing she found was a pretty tin box which was just what she needed for her postcard collection. She stowed the box in her wheelbarrow.

Then she saw something red in the sand. It was a rug with one corner missing, but it would look just lovely in her bedroom. The torn end could be tucked under a chest, so she stowed the rug in her wheelbarrow.

She next came upon a pile of driftwood. What beautiful colors it would make burning in her fireplace! There was too much for one load, so she stowed as much as she could in her wheelbarrow and headed home. She would come back for the rest later.

Captain Kidd was the first to see the deep purple bottle and he didn't like it at all. It was closed tight and these words were scratched on it: *Do Not Open.*

As Miss Moody picked up the bottle, a voice said, "What do you want more than anything in the world?"

More than anything in the world, Miss Moody wanted her banjo clock to run: to tick and bong like banjo clocks are supposed to do. She was certainly not about to tell this to a stranger. "None of your beeswax!" she snapped and turned around to see who had sneaked up behind her.

No one was anywhere in sight. She couldn't even see Captain Kidd for a moment, and then she noticed his tail twitching from under the wheelbarrow.

"I'll give you whatever you want if you'll just let me out, please."

The voice was coming from the bottle! Miss Moody almost dropped it. "Who are you?" she demanded.

"I'm a poor little child. I was put in here by a wicked person and now I want to go home to my mama. Pull out the stopper and please free me!"

Should she open the bottle? Miss Moody could not stand hearing a child cry. She tugged at the stopper, and suddenly the stopper popped out.

Smoke started to trickle out of the bottle, so Miss Moody threw the bottle on the sand. The smoke came out in billows, twisting into a big black cloud, and then the bottle broke. From inside the cloud came terrible laughter. It was not the laughter of a child.

"Free!" roared a voice like thunder.

The smoke cleared away and Miss Moody was staring at the biggest, ugliest creature she had ever seen.

"Thank you, madam," it said. "Too bad you didn't make a wish. You could have had anything you wanted—gold, gems, a palace. I could have made you a queen or a president."

"You are just a bad, bad dream," Miss Moody said.

"Why aren't you afraid of me?" the creature asked.

"Because I'm not afraid of anything I don't believe in, and I don't believe in you for a minute."

The creature grew bigger and uglier. "Now are you afraid of me?" it demanded.

"No," said Miss Moody.

The creature grew even bigger and even uglier. "Are you still not afraid of me?" it growled.

"Getting bigger and uglier doesn't scare me," said Miss Moody. "I'm only afraid of mice, and you can't grow small like a little mouse."

The creature disappeared. At Miss Moody's feet was a tiny gray mouse.

Captain Kidd jumped so quickly the mouse didn't have time to squeak. He swallowed it.

"Captain!" cried Miss Moody. "Are you all right?"

Captain Kidd stretched. Miss Moody, Captain Kidd, and the wheelbarrow all went home, shaking a little bit.

Before they got to the cottage, Miss Moody heard it: "Bong! bong! bong! bong! bong! bong! bong! bong!" She rushed inside.

The handsome banjo clock over the fireplace was ticking away busily. The hands pointed to one minute past eight o'clock.

1. How was Miss Moody's trip to the beach after this storm different from her other trips?

2. How did Miss Moody solve her problem at the beach?

3. There was another surprise waiting for Miss Moody when she got home. What was it?

4. How do you think Miss Moody felt when she got home?

5. When did you know the creature wouldn't hurt Miss Moody?

Read the conclusion below. Decide which of the details below support the conclusion.

Conclusion: Miss Moody wasn't afraid of things that might frighten other people.

1. Miss Moody loved storms.

2. The big ugly creature didn't scare Miss Moody.

3. Miss Moody wanted her banjo clock to run.

Prewrite

Think about all the things Miss Moody had found on the beach after the storms. Which of these things do you think is the most interesting? If you took a walk on the beach after a storm, what might you find?

Compose

Choose one of the activities below.

1. Pretend that you have just taken a walk on the beach after a terrible storm. Write a paragraph describing something you might find on the beach. Tell why you might decide to keep it.

2. Suppose that you have just found the purple bottle marked "Do Not Open." Write a paragraph that tells what you will do with the bottle. Will you open it? Will you make a wish? What might happen next?

Revise

Read your paragraph. Did you describe what happened clearly? Make changes that are needed.

Many living things can be found on a beach. Read to find out what some of these living things are.

Beach Life

by Louisa Johnston

A beach, or shore, is the land along the edge of a body of water. A sea, an ocean, a river, and a lake all have a beach made of rock, mud, or sand. The sand on a beach was once large rocks and seashells that over a period of many, many years were pounded down by the wind and the water into very tiny bits or grains.

A beach is the home of a great number of living things, and it is a good place to explore and study them. High tide, or the rise of the tide, is when the water moves up onto the beach in waves. As the water moves along the shore, it carries living and non-living things with it. After some time, the tide begins to fall and the water moves back down to a lower level, or low tide. During the rise and fall of tides, many living and non-living things are left on the beach. This happens twice each day.

A storm is also a time when living and non-living things are pulled up by the current and left along the beach. Some of the living things left on the beach are animals such as crabs, shellfish, and starfish. Seaweed and other plants can also be found. Some of the non-living things that can be found on the beach are empty shells, rocks, and driftwood.

The beach is also a home for plants, as well as sand and sea animals. These living things are able to live together, take care of one another, and respect each other. Each animal or plant fits into a special place in its home and touches the life of every other thing that lives around it. Empty shells, rocks, and driftwood act to protect the plants, the sand animals, and the sea animals from things that might harm or even kill them.

Did you ever move a rock or pick up a shell and discover the home of a small sea animal? A hermit crab will often find the empty shell of another sea animal and use it for a home. Inside the shell, the hermit crab will be safe from strong winds, rough currents, other animals, and even people.

Since the beach is a good place to visit, many people go there to swim, fish, sail, and picnic. People can do the most good for beach animals by respecting them and their homes. People can do their share to get along with sea life and to help keep the beach beautiful.

The beach is a place you can enjoy with all your senses. Use your sense of touch as you walk along the edge of the water and feel the sand under your bare feet and between your toes. You can almost taste the salt from the water, and you can smell the fresh sea air. Hear the sound of the waves slapping against the shore. Watch carefully for animals that live in the sand and water. Life and color and unusual shapes are on a sandy beach waiting for you to explore them.

1. What are some of the living things that can be found on a beach?

2. Why do people find the beach interesting?

3. What is the best time to see the most sea life?

4. Why do you think you might like the beach at low tide?

5. What helps you know what your senses are?

The main idea of a paragraph or selection is the most important idea. Often details support, or tell about, the main idea.

Read the main idea and supporting detail below. Then find two more details in the selection that support this main idea.

Main idea: The beach is the home of many living and non-living things.

Detail: Seaweed and other plants can also be found.

Prewrite

Think about the fun you could have at the beach. What could you do? What might you see? What discoveries might you make?

Compose

Choose one of the activities below.

1. Pretend that you are at the beach on vacation. Write a letter to a friend telling about your vacation. Tell what you have been doing at the beach. Follow the rules for writing a friendly letter.

2. Reread the last paragraph of the selection. Write a paragraph that answers the following questions: What could you see at the beach? What could you hear? What could you feel? What could you taste? What could you smell? Write about things different from those listed in the selection.

Revise

Read your work. Did you follow the directions? Make changes that are needed.

Author's Purpose

Authors write for many reasons. Often they write about real or make-believe people, places, or events that may be funny, sad, or scary. Sometimes authors write about these things **to entertain** you. Authors also write about these things **to inform** you by giving facts or ideas.

The following paragraphs were written to entertain. Read them and tell how you know this was the author's purpose.

When he finished with unpacking, Nelson walked over to Adam Joshua's closet to put his suitcases away. Adam Joshua's pile of piles fell out all over him the minute he opened the door.

"Adam Joshua!" yelled Nelson, shaking a toy dinosaur off his foot. "This is no way to treat a friend!"

from *The Kid Next Door and Other Headaches*
by Janice Lee Smith

94

The author is describing Nelson, who is upset with his friend Adam Joshua. You may laugh when you try to imagine a pile of clothes and toys falling out of the closet as Nelson opens the door.

The next paragraph was written to inform. Read it and tell how you know that this was the author's purpose.

Where the land meets the sea we find seashells. There are many different kinds of shells. They can be round like the moon, long like a jackknife, or shaped like boxes, fans, or tops. The shells we find are usually empty, but once there were soft bodies inside. Animals with hard shells outside and soft bodies inside are called mollusks.

from *A First Look at Seashells*
by Millicent E. Selsam and Joyce Hunt

The author is sharing facts and information about seashells. You should have learned something about seashells if you did not know anything about them before reading the paragraph.

After you have read a selection, try to decide why the author wrote it. Was the author's main purpose to share information or to entertain you?

A treasure hunt on the beach is a way for Elisabeth and Charles to learn about things that live there. What are some of the things that Elisabeth and Charles learn?

Elisabeth the Treasure Hunter

(adapted from a story)
by Felice Holman

Elisabeth's mother packed a "treasure" in a tin box so Elisabeth could be a treasure hunter. Elisabeth's father was going to bury the treasure on the beach and give Elisabeth some clues to help her find it. When Elisabeth and her father got to the beach, they met Professor Eckleberry and his grandson, Charles. They asked the professor to bury the treasure for them and give them some clues. Charles decided that he wanted to help Elisabeth and her father find the treasure.

"Let's take a look at the clue," Papa said.

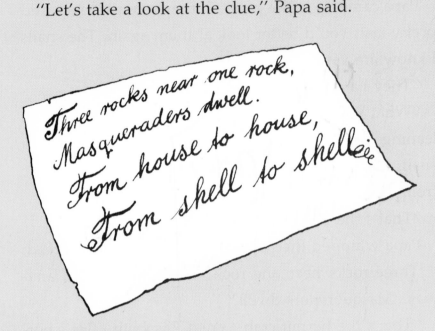

Three rocks near one rock,
Masqueraders dwell.
From house to house,
From shell to shell.

"That means we will find something or other, in or near something, that is near three rocks, that are near one rock," said Papa.

They walked along, and then Elisabeth called, "Here are three big rocks at the edge of the water!"

Then Charles said, "There's one rock all by itself farther up on the shore."

Elisabeth and Charles ran down to the edge of the water. The rocks stood like mountains around a small pool of water.

"It's full of snails," said Elisabeth, "and they're walking around pretty fast."

Papa came up to the pool. "If they're walking around pretty fast, you'd better look at them again. The snails I know are very slow-moving."

"They have awfully long legs," Charles said.

"What you have found is a hermit crab," said Papa leaning over the pool. "His shell once belonged to a snail. He has no shell of his own so he borrows one from a snail and uses it for a house."

"That's the clue!" cried Charles.

Papa whipped the paper out of his pocket. He read: " 'Three rocks near one rock.' Well, that's right, anyway. 'Masqueraders dwell?' "

"That's the hermit crab!" cried Elisabeth. "He's borrowed a snail's shell. Hey, look at that! There's a piece of paper in the pool, partly hidden under a shell."

Charles reached into the pool for the paper. Papa took the wet piece of paper from Charles.

Papa frowned. "It says:"

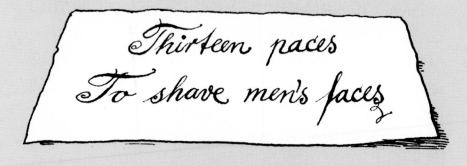

Thirteen paces
To shave men's faces

"It does say 'thirteen paces.' Let's walk and count our steps," Papa said.

Charles took the biggest steps he could, and counted thirteen paces. Elisabeth didn't get as far. Papa's paces took him farthest of all because his legs were the longest.

"All right now," Papa called, "let's look around and see what will shave men's faces."

They formed their line again and walked along, heads down, looking closely at the wet sand.

"Tide's coming in," Papa said. "We'll have to hurry. Charles, your grandfather said the clues were only good for an hour."

"Look at this funny, sharp shell sticking out of the sand," said Charles.

"Here's another," declared Elisabeth.

"These clams are called razor clams. See, this empty shell is shaped like an old-fashioned razor," said Papa.

"Razors!" exclaimed Elisabeth.

"Exactly," said Papa. " 'Thirteen paces to shave men's faces.' Look! I was just turning over this razor-clam shell, and there on the shell . . . do you see what I see?"

"It's another clue!" cried Elisabeth.

Papa looked closely at the shell, and read:

*Little feathers lead the way
To beads of white on rocks of gray*

Charles started walking in a way that reminded Elisabeth of a tightrope walker in the circus, putting one foot in front of the other and balancing with his arms.

"What are you doing?" she asked.

"I'm following the footsteps," he declared. Elisabeth looked down and saw some faint tracks in the sand.

"A gull has made those faint tracks," said Papa.

"They're very feathery footprints," declared Elisabeth.

"Feathery!" exclaimed Charles. *"Feathers!"*

" 'Little *feathers* lead the way . . .' " said Elisabeth. "Let's follow the gull tracks!"

The gull tracks led down the shore and to the stone jetty. Charles and Elisabeth climbed up onto the nearest of the large rocks.

"Look!" Charles called. "The jetty is covered with thousands of little white cabbages. Ow! They're sharp!"

"They look like beads to me," said Elisabeth.

"What kind of beads?" asked Papa.

"White beads," said Elisabeth.

" 'Beads of white,' " Papa said.

" 'Rocks of gray,' " Charles added.

"The clue!" cried Elisabeth.

"What are beads doing here on the rock?" asked Charles.

"Well," Papa said, "although these look like beads, they are really a small animal called a barnacle. Many of them are closed up tightly over a little, upside-down animal that is waiting for the sea to come back."

"There are barnacles on this rope, too," Charles declared, tugging on a rope he found in the water.

"Papa!" cried Elisabeth. "Charles! It's our tin box! It's the treasure tied to the end of this rope!"

"Maybe the tide came up over it," said Charles.

"Here, let me help," Papa said.

Inside the box everything was dry as could be, and there was the treasure, looking very good. There were large chunks of gold, looking like beautiful peaches; pieces of jade, looking like bunches of grapes shining in the sun; and beautiful gems, looking like red, yellow, and green apples.

"The tide is coming in quickly, now. We'd better be moving off the rocks," Papa said. He led them down onto the sand.

"If we eat the treasure we found, we will have no treasure left," said Elisabeth.

Elisabeth looked at the beach and down at her feet where the water was running onto the shore. She saw the little creatures the tide was bringing in and leaving on the beach.

"Do you know what?" Elisabeth said. "The beach is a kind of treasure, isn't it?"

1. How do Elisabeth and Charles learn about the things that live on the beach?

2. What does Elisabeth discover about the beach?

3. What do Elisabeth, Papa, and Charles do once they find their treasure?

4. What do you think about the clues?

5. When did you know that the treasure hunt would be more fun than Elisabeth's mother had planned?

Apply the Skills

Read each group of sentences below. Decide if it was written to inform or to entertain.

1. The hermit crab's shell once belonged to a snail. He has no shell of his own so he borrows one from the snail.

2. "Papa!" cried Elisabeth. "Charles! It's our tin box! It's the treasure tied to the end of this rope!"

104

Prewrite

In "Elisabeth the Treasure Hunter," Elisabeth searched for treasure on the beach. As Elisabeth and Charles followed Professor Eckleberry's clues to the buried treasure, they discovered other things. Could these things be called a "treasure"? Why?

Compose

Choose one of the activities below.

1. In a paragraph, describe one of the discoveries Elisabeth and Charles made while they searched for the buried treasure.

2. The buried treasure Elisabeth and Charles found looked like gold, jade, and beautiful gems. Write a paragraph that tells what the treasure really was and why it might have looked so wonderful to Elisabeth and Charles.

Revise

Check your work carefully. Will your paragraph make sense to the person reading it? If changes are needed, make them.

Until I Saw the Sea

by Lilian Moore

Until I saw the sea
I did not know
that wind
could wrinkle water so.

I never knew
that sun
could splinter a whole sea of blue.

Nor
did I know before,
a sea breathes in and out
upon a shore.

Dictionary

A dictionary is a useful tool for finding the definition or meaning of a word. A dictionary can also help you spell words and tell you how to pronounce them. A dictionary, just like an encyclopedia, is arranged in alphabetical order.

Three important parts of a dictionary page are

1. entry words,

2. guide words,

3. pronunciation key.

---

giant

giraffe

gi·ant [jī'ənt] **1** *n.* An imaginary being in human form but a great deal larger and more powerful than a real person. **2** *n.* Any person, animal, or thing of great size, strength, intelligence or ability. **3** *adj.* Huge or great.

gib·bon [gib'ən] *n.* A slender, long-armed ape of SE Asia and the East Indies, that lives in trees.

gift [gift] *n.* **1** Something that is given; present. **2** A natural ability; talent: a *gift* for music.

gig·gle [gig'əl] *v.* **gig·gled, gig·gling,** *n.* **1** *v.* To laugh in a silly or nervous manner with high fluttering sounds. **2** *n.* Such a laugh. —**gig' gler** *n.*

Gi·la monster [hē'lə] A large, poisonous lizard of the SW U.S. and northern Mexico. It is covered with black and orange scales.

gin·ger·snap [jin'jər·snap'] *n.* A small, flat, brittle cookie flavored with ginger and molasses.

ging·ham [ging'əm] *n.* A cotton fabric woven in solid colors, stripes, checks, or plaids. *Gingham* goes back to a Malay word meaning *striped.*

gi·raffe [jə·raf'] *n.* An African animal that chews its cud. The tallest of all animals living today, it has a very long neck, long slender legs, and a spotted skin.

a	add	i	it	o͝o	took	oi	oil
ā	ace	ī	ice	o͞o	pool	ou	pout
â	care	o	odd	u	up	ng	ring
ä	palm	ō	open	û	burn	th	thin
e	end	ô	order	yo͞o	fuse	t̶h̶	this
ē	equal					zh	vision

ə = { a in *above*   e in *sicken*   i in *possible*
      o in *melon*   u in *circus* }

Gila monster

Entry Words

Find the words *giant, gift,* and *giggle* on the sample dictionary page. These words are printed in boldface and are listed in alphabetical order on the page. These and all the other boldface words on the page are the **entry words.** When you use the dictionary, look for the entry words.

Guide Words

Look at the two words *giant* and *giraffe* printed in blue at the top of the dictionary page. These are the **guide words** for this page. They tell you that the first entry word on the page is *giant* and that the last entry word is *giraffe.* All the other entry words on the page will be in alphabetical order between these two guide words. Guide words are a useful way of quickly finding entry words.

Pronunciation Key

Look at the entry word *giant.* Next to it in brackets [ ], *giant* is respelled with letters and symbols that help you pronounce the word. To understand the sounds these symbols stand for, you need to use the **pronunciation key.** A short form of the key is usually shown at the bottom of the dictionary page. The full pronunciation key is always found at the front of the book.

Using Guide Words and Entry Words

The guide words on the sample dictionary page are *giant* and *giraffe*. Suppose you want to find the following words in the dictionary. Which would be on the same page with the guide words *giant* and *giraffe*?

gill, give, get, ginger

The words *gill* and *ginger* would be on the page because the letters *gil* and *gin* come after the first three letters of the guide word *giant* and before the first three letters of the guide word *giraffe*. The word *get* would not be on the same page because *get* comes before *giant* in alphabetical order. The word *give* would not be on that page because *give* comes after *giraffe* in alphabetical order.

Guide words are an important part of a dictionary page. By using alphabetical order and the guide words, you will find entry words more quickly than if you read every entry word on the page.

Look at the entry word *flipper* on the next page. Notice that it is printed in boldface type. Notice the numerals *1* and *2* in the definition for *flipper*. These numerals tell you that there are two meanings for the word. Which definition matches the way the word *flipper* is used in the sentence below the definition of *flipper*? Why?

> **flip·per** [flip′ər] *n.* **1** A broad, flat limb, as of a seal, adapted for swimming. **2** A broad, flat shoe like a fin, worn by skin divers.

The swimmer put on a mask and flippers before getting into the water.

The second definition fits the sentence because the meaning of the word *flipper* has to do with something a person puts on to help him or her swim.

Read the following entry words and their definitions. Then read the sentence under each. Decide which definition best fits the meaning of the word as it is used in the sentence.

> **dol·ly** [dol′ē] *n.* **1** A doll: a child's term. **2** A low, flat frame set on small wheels or rollers, used for moving heavy loads.

The band used the dolly to move the instruments.

> **sid·ing** [sī′ding] *n.* **1** A railroad track by the side of the main track, onto which cars may be switched. **2** A material, as overlapping boards, used to construct the outside walls of a house or building with a wooden frame.

After the siding on the house was painted, the house looked brand new.

Remember to use guide words to help you find a word quickly. Once you find the entry word, read all the definitions. Try each definition with the sentence in which the word appears. Then decide which definition best fits the word that is used in the sentence.

Jimmy and some other children are on a spaceship. What is Jimmy hoping to see as he looks out the portholes?

In Space

by George Zebrowski

"What are we going to do?" Jimmy's brother asked. They were waiting for Jimmy to come up with a plan, or they would be left to drift in space forever.

Jimmy Wilson knew that his brother, Billy, and the six others were frightened. Suddenly he felt much older than any of them. They were all under ten. He was going to be thirteen. If he lived to see February 24, 2095, that is. Way down deep, Jimmy didn't feel all that much older than the others. It just seemed that way now, as he looked at their faces.

Turning away from Billy and the others, Jimmy remembered all that had happened. He thought of the wonderful summer he had spent on Lea, the Earth-like planet. Then he remembered how he had gotten on the large space liner and had taken off on the return flight to Earth. Jimmy had been on the ship's deck when everything began. The captain had told them that the ship's engines were out of control and could not be fixed. The engines would explode before they reached Earth.

Next, Jimmy thought about how one of the ship's officers had directed him, Billy, and the others onto the liner's lifeboat. Before the officer could get on himself, the metal door had closed. Then the engines of the lifeboat had started, and it had pulled away from the liner. Jimmy and the others had drifted farther and farther away from the liner, and then the liner had exploded.

"What are we going to do?" Billy asked again. Jimmy turned around and looked at his brother. Jimmy said nothing. Standing with his back to the control panel, Jimmy looked around the tiny room. On the gray metal walls were two portholes made of heavy plastic. Jimmy looked out through the one to his right. The stars looked cold.

There were eight children altogether. Besides Billy and himself, there were Tammy Wong and her brother, Jack; a little boy named Frankie; Patty and Sammy Gold; and the youngest, Albert Cohen.

"Sit still, all of you!" Jimmy said suddenly. "I'm going to check the controls now, so be quiet."

Jimmy turned and sat down in the control seat. All the lights on the panel were on—except one. The small sign under it read: *Emergency Sighting Light. When this light turns green, you are near a rescue ship. Push button to return signal.* This way Jimmy would know when help was near.

Then Jimmy saw a button with the word *Screen* under it. He pushed the button, and a screen lit up showing a picture of space. Jimmy couldn't understand the other buttons. "If only the ship's officer were here," Jimmy thought.

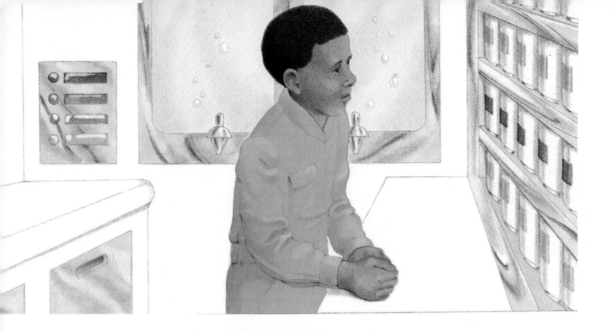

As Jimmy got up from the control seat, he thought of food. "How much is there?" he wondered. Slowly, he made his way back to the back of the control room. He opened the door to the ship's kitchen. He found dozens of cans of food, plus many large tanks of drinking water. Jimmy had no idea how long the food and water might last.

The tiny control room had four bunks that opened down from the wall. Jimmy's seven passengers climbed into the bunks to sleep. Jimmy watched them from the control seat, where he planned to sleep. "Soon," he thought, "their parents will be wondering what has happened to them. Well, I'm the oldest, and I'll take care of them."

The next day, Jimmy went into the kitchen to get some food. Billy followed him. "What's going to happen to us, Jimmy?" he asked.

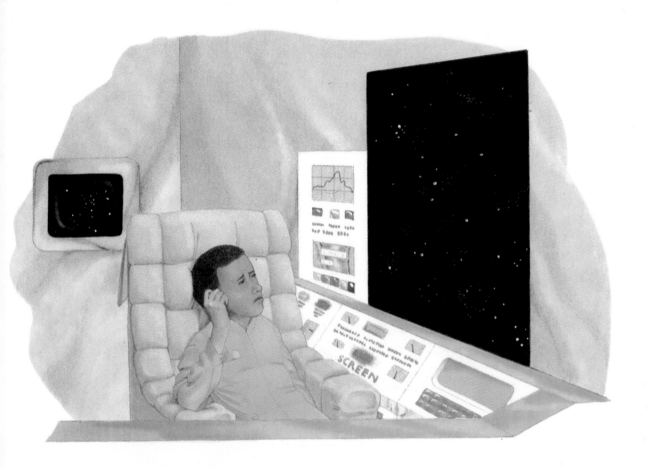

"Wait, Billy. Don't ask me now."

By the sixth day after the wreck of the liner, Jimmy still tried not to show that he was scared. The food was going much faster than he had thought it would. There was still plenty of water, but in nine or ten days, all the food would be gone. "What will I do then?" Jimmy wondered. "What will I tell the others?"

Jimmy kept watching the emergency sighting light, hoping that it would come on. It never did. It was always dark. When he looked up at the screen, Jimmy saw that the stars had not changed.

On the thirteenth day, Jimmy woke up slowly. The others had been awake for some time, but they were still lying in their bunks. They had stopped playing a long time ago, it seemed. While some of them cried, others stayed quiet.

Jimmy got up and went to the kitchen for some food. When he saw that there was only enough left for three more days, he thought he would have to stop eating. He was bigger and stronger than the others. They needed the food more than he did.

Jimmy gave everyone some food. No one noticed that he took nothing.

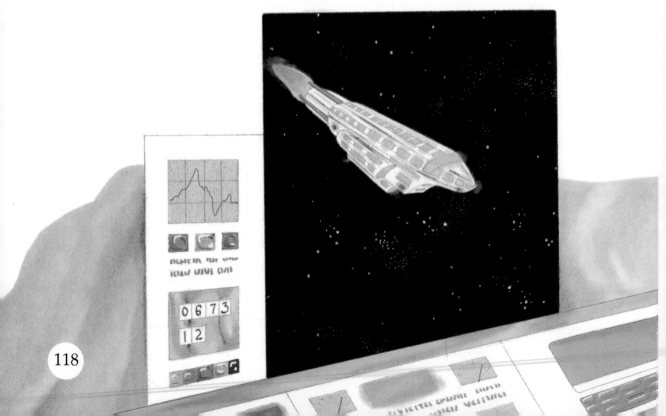

When the lifeboat had been in space for seventeen days, the eight children inside were hungry and weak. There was no more food left from the dozens of cans that had been there. While the others cried, Jimmy thought about how happy he had been during the vacation on Lea. Everyone had laughed then. All that was gone now, as if it had never been.

With tears in his eyes, Jimmy looked up at the screen. Nothing had changed. "No one will come for us out of that darkness," Jimmy thought. "There are too many stars for us to get lost in."

Suddenly, Jimmy thought he saw the green light go on. "Do something, Jimmy!" shouted Billy. Jimmy leaned forward and pushed the button. As he watched the screen, waiting to see the rescue ship, he thought the stars looked almost friendly now. Jimmy looked at the screen. There was the rescue ship. Everything would soon be over.

119

1. What was Jimmy hoping to see when he looked out the portholes and at the screen?

2. What were some of the problems the children had on the lifeboat?

3. How did Jimmy know the rescue ship was coming?

4. Do you think Jimmy should have felt that he had to take care of the other children? Why?

5. When did you know the children were on their own in the lifeboat?

Apply the Skills

Below are six words from the story. Put the words in alphabetical order as if they were entry words on a dictionary page.

drift   control   engine   deck   explode   dozens

What would be the guide words on this page?

Prewrite

Think about the space adventure you have just read. Would this be the kind of adventure you would enjoy? Imagine yourself on a space adventure. What might happen? How would a trip on an ocean ship be different?

Compose

Choose one of the activities below.

1. Imagine that you have been named captain of a spaceship. Write a short story telling about an adventure in space. You may also wish to give a description of your spaceship.

2. How are an ocean ship and a spaceship alike? How are they different? Write a paragraph that tells two ways they are alike and two ways they are different.

Revise

Read what you have written. Be sure to make it interesting to the person reading it. If changes are needed, make them.

Context Clues

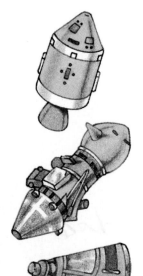

Astronauts have exciting jobs as space travelers.

Read the above sentence. What does the word *astronauts* mean? If you did not know the meaning of *astronauts,* what words in the sentence might help you? Notice the words *space travelers* in the sentence. These words help you know that astronauts are people who travel in space. The context, the other words in the sentence, gave you the clue to the meaning of *astronauts.*

Context clues may be in the same sentence as the word, or they may be in other sentences around the word. Read the sentences that follow.

Maria visited a space museum with her class and saw many kinds of spaceships. She liked the exhibit of rockets the best.

If you did not know the meaning of *rockets,* other words around it would help you. The words *space museum* tell you that the rockets were in a museum for space objects. The words *many kinds of spaceships* tell you that rockets are a kind of spaceship.

Sometimes a definition may be given in the same sentence as the word. Words such as *is, means, meant, called,* and *or* often signal that a definition is going to be given. Read the following sentences. What does *astronomy* mean? How do you know?

- Astronomy is the study of the stars, planets, and other heavenly bodies.

- Astronomy means "the study of the stars, planets, and other heavenly bodies."

- The study of the stars, planets, and other heavenly bodies, called astronomy, is of great interest to him.

- The study of the stars, planets, and other heavenly bodies, or astronomy, is of great interest to her.

Each sentence tells the definition of astronomy. The words *is, means, called* and *or* are clues that the sentence context contains the definition.

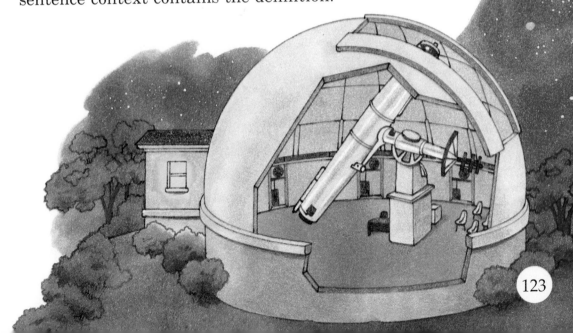

Textbook Application: Using Context Clues in Science

Many of the words in a science book are defined or explained in the context. Read the following article from a science book. Use the sidenotes to help you.

These two sentences help you know what planets are.

The context of this sentence defines *solar system.*

What is the meaning of the word *orbit*? What word signals that definition?

You are in a spaceship far out in space. In the distance, you can see the Sun. It glows with a bright yellow light. Near the Sun are nine other bodies in space. These bodies are called planets. The planets move around the Sun. They spin like tops, too. The Sun and the planets make up our solar system.

Each planet that you see is traveling around the Sun. Each travels in its own path, called an orbit. Some planets travel fast. Others travel slowly. They take a long, long time to complete one orbit around the Sun. Our journey starts now. Our ship will travel through the solar system.

—*HBJ Science*, Harcourt Brace Jovanovich

Read the paragraph that follows. Use context clues to find out the meaning of the words *astronomer, telescope, satellites,* and *comets.* Notice that signal words are given for some of the context clues.

A person who studies the objects in the night sky is an astronomer. An astronomer uses a telescope to see far into the distance. This instrument makes the stars and planets look bigger. Some of the planets have satellites, or moons, around them. Sometimes frozen bodies of dust, called comets, are seen.

Did you notice that signal words were given to help you know the meaning of *astronomer, satellites,* and *comets?* Did you also notice that no signal words were given for the meaning of *telescope?* The context of sentences two and three helps you know the meaning of *telescope.* The clues in these sentences are *to see far into the distance* and *instrument makes the stars and planets look bigger.*

As you read and come to a word whose meaning you are not sure of, remember to look for context clues. Remember that context clues may be in the same sentence as the word, or they may be in other sentences around the word.

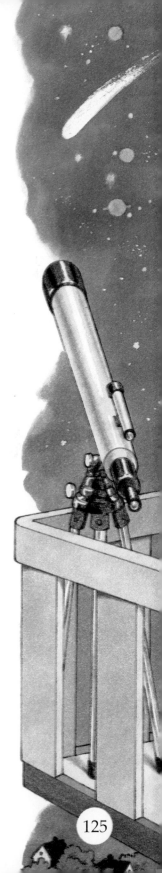

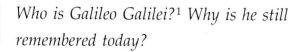

Who is Galileo Galilei?[1] Why is he still remembered today?

Galileo

by Arthur S. Gregor

From the time Galileo Galilei was a boy, he thought about the stars and wondered about them. Galileo's father, who let him stay up late to look at the sky filled with thousands of stars, couldn't answer all the boy's questions.

---

[1] Galileo Galilei [gal′ə•lē′ō gal′ə•lā′ē]

"What are they made of?" Galileo cried. "Where did they come from? Will they go away?"

His father laughed. "Always asking questions, aren't you? When you are a student, you will read the books of those who are wise. There you will find some of the answers."

Galileo was a very good student in school. When he was seventeen years old, he went from Florence, Italy, to the city of Pisa[1] to study medicine. Galileo liked to ask questions about many things he saw around him. He soon found out that he did not want to be a doctor. He knew he wanted to be a scientist.

Galileo's mind jumped from thinking about the earth to thinking about the moon, the sun, the stars, and the planets. Galileo became the father of space science when he proved that things in space did move because there was nothing to get in their way. Today this discovery is used when a satellite goes into space.

In 1604, a new star was found in the sky. It glowed yellow, purple, red, and white. It was so bright it could be seen during the day. The star shone for one-and-one-half years, and then it faded and disappeared. While it blazed, people wondered about it. "A new star is not possible," people told Galileo.

---

[1] Pisa [pē′zə]

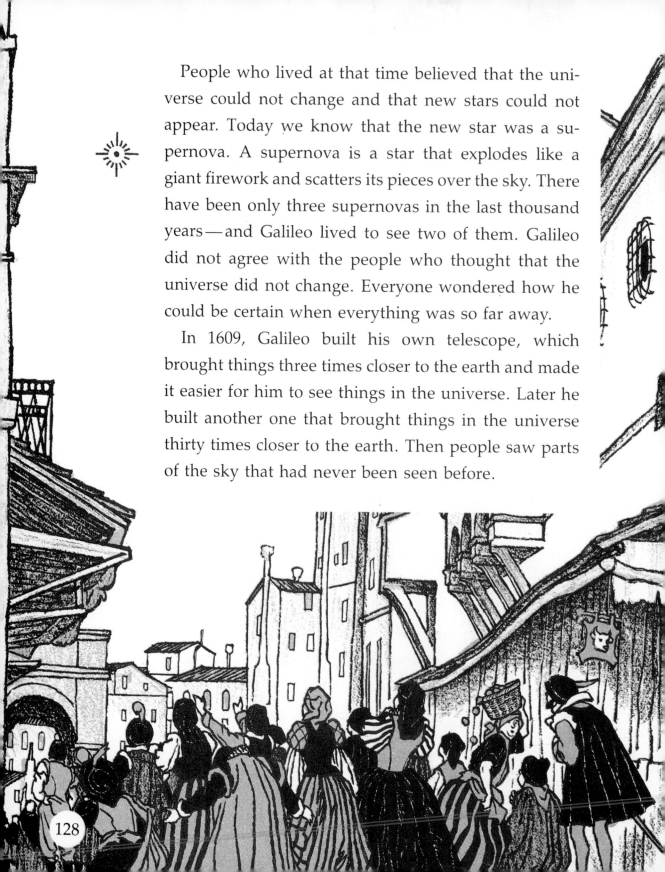

People who lived at that time believed that the universe could not change and that new stars could not appear. Today we know that the new star was a supernova. A supernova is a star that explodes like a giant firework and scatters its pieces over the sky. There have been only three supernovas in the last thousand years—and Galileo lived to see two of them. Galileo did not agree with the people who thought that the universe did not change. Everyone wondered how he could be certain when everything was so far away.

In 1609, Galileo built his own telescope, which brought things three times closer to the earth and made it easier for him to see things in the universe. Later he built another one that brought things in the universe thirty times closer to the earth. Then people saw parts of the sky that had never been seen before.

With the new telescope, Galileo made many discoveries. He found that the Milky Way was not a cloud, but a great cluster of stars. He saw that the moon was not perfectly smooth and round. He also discovered that there were moons going around Jupiter, just as our moon travels around the earth.

Galileo knew his work was just the beginning. He knew some day others would explore the rest of the universe. Galileo was right. There are astronomers who are studying outer space today using Galileo's discoveries. The astronauts, too, depend on the first great scientist of modern times—Galileo Galilei.

1. What did Galileo do that made him famous?
2. Why is it important to know about Galileo?
3. How does Galileo's discovery—that things move in space—help us today?
4. What do you think about Galileo's discoveries?
5. What told you that Galileo was able to prove that the universe changes?

Guide words are at the top of a dictionary page. The entry words on a page are in alphabetical order between the two guide words. From the guide words and entry words below, select the one entry word that goes between each pair of guide words.

1. Guide Words: safety ▬▬▬ space

   Entry Word: supernova *or* satellite

2. Guide Words: apple ▬▬▬ attic

   Entry Word: astronaut *or* answer

Prewrite

The words below are from the story "Galileo." Think about what each word means.

scientist   universe

satellite   telescope

Compose

Choose one word from the list above. Write two sentences that use context clues to define the word. Remember, *context clues* are words in a sentence or paragraph that help you understand the meaning of another word. For example, the word *supernova* is defined in the selection like this:

A supernova is a star that explodes like a giant firework display and scatters its pieces over the sky.

Revise

Check your work to make sure you have correctly defined the word you have chosen. Use a dictionary if you are unsure of the definition. Make changes that are needed.

My Star
by Marion Kennedy

In a sky of black velvet
The silver stars shine.
I think I'll choose one
And pretend it is mine.
I'll choose one that twinkles
And winks down at me;
Then snug in my bed every
Night I shall see
My very own star shining
Far overhead,
And winking good night to me,
Curled up in bed.

A selfish giant learns that he should share what he has with others. How does the giant learn this?

The Selfish Giant

by Oscar Wilde

Every afternoon, as they were coming from school, the children used to go and play in the Giant's garden. It was a large garden, with soft green grass. Here and there over the grass stood beautiful flowers like stars. There were twelve peach trees that in the springtime broke out into soft blossoms of pink and white. In the autumn the garden held rich fruit. The birds sat on the trees and sang. The children used to stop their games in order to listen to them. "How happy we are here!" they cried to each other.

One day the Giant came back. He had been to visit
his friend, and had stayed with him for seven years.
After the seven years were over, the Giant wanted to
return to his own castle. When he arrived, he saw
the children playing in the garden.

"What are you doing there?" the Giant demanded
in a very gruff voice, and the children ran away.

"My own garden is my own garden," said the
Giant. "Anyone can understand that. I will allow
nobody to play in it but myself." So the Selfish Giant
built a high wall all around it and put up a sign telling the children to stay away. The poor children now
had nowhere to play.

Then Spring came, and all over the country there were little blossoms and little birds. Only in the garden of the Selfish Giant it was still winter. The birds did not care to sing, and the trees forgot to blossom.

The only people who were really pleased were Snow and Frost. "Spring has forgotten this garden," they cried. "We will live here all the year round." Snow covered up the grass with his great white cloak, and Frost painted all the trees silver. Then North Wind came to stay.

Hail came next. Every day for three hours he rattled on the roof of the castle till he broke most of the slates. Hail was dressed in gray, and his breath was like ice.

"I cannot understand why Spring is so late in coming," said the Selfish Giant, as he sat at the window and looked out at his cold, white garden. "I hope there will be a change in the weather."

Spring never came, and Summer never came. Autumn gave golden fruit to every garden but the Giant's. "The Giant is much too selfish," Autumn said. So it was always winter there, and North Wind, and Hail, and Frost, and Snow danced about through the trees.

One morning the Giant was lying awake in bed
when he heard some lovely music. It was a bird singing sweetly outside his window. It was so long since
he had heard a bird sing in his garden that it seemed
to him to be the most glorious music in the world.
Then Hail stopped dancing, and North Wind stopped
roaring. "I believe Spring has come at last," said the
Giant. He jumped out of bed and looked out. What
did he see?

He saw a most wonderful sight. Through a little hole in the wall, the children had crept in, and they were sitting in the branches of the trees. In every tree that the Giant could see, there was a little child. The trees were so glad to have the children back again that they had covered themselves with blossoms. They were waving their arms softly above the children's heads. The birds were flying about and singing with delight. The flowers were looking up through the green grass and laughing.

It was a lovely picture, only in one corner it was still winter. It was the farthest corner of the garden, and in it was standing a timid little boy. He was so small that he could not reach up to the branches of the tree. He was crying. The poor tree was still covered with frost and snow, and North Wind was blowing and roaring above it. "Climb up! little boy," said Tree, and it bent its branches down as low as it could. The boy was too tiny.

The Giant's heart melted as he looked out. "How selfish I have been!" he said. "Now I know why Spring would not come here. I will put that timid little boy on the top of the tree, and then I will knock down the wall. My garden shall be the children's playground for ever and ever." He was really very sorry for what he had done.

So he went downstairs and opened the front door quite softly, and went out into the garden. The Giant placed the timid boy in the tree. At once, the tree blossomed, and the birds came and sang.

"It is your garden now, little children," said the Giant. He took a great ax and knocked down the wall. When the people were going to market at twelve o'clock, they found the Giant playing with the children in the most glorious garden they had ever seen.

1. How did the Giant learn that he should share with others?

2. Why did the Giant's garden begin to bloom again?

3. Why did the Giant knock down the garden wall?

4. What did you think had happened when the Giant heard the bird sing?

5. When did you know the Giant had made a mistake when he built the wall?

Apply the Skills

Sequence helps us understand a story. When we read, we need to know what happens first and what happens next. The author uses words such as *then one day, finally, seven years later,* and *next* to help us understand the sequence.

On pages 135 and 136 of your story, find examples of time clues the author uses to tell when things happened. Look for five examples.

Prewrite

Personification means "making a thing seem as if it is a person and can do things a person can do." The following examples of personification are from the story.

> Snow covered up the grass with his great white cloak, and Frost painted all the trees silver.

Compose

Choose one of the activities below.

1. Look for examples of personification in the story. Write down two examples and tell what characteristics the author has given them to make them seem like people.

2. Make up two examples of personification and write them down. Tell what characteristic you gave to each thing to make it seem as if it were a person.

Revise

Read what you have written. Make any changes that are needed.

My Dad Is Really Something

by Lois Osborn

Ron is a new boy in my class. I like him a lot, but sometimes he makes me mad.

One day I showed the kids at school a book my dad had written. Then Ron had to speak up.

"Aw, that's nothing, Harry George," he said. "You should see what my father can do. He can tear a phone book in half with his bare hands. I bet your father can't do that."

When I got home, I gave the phone book to my dad. I told him what Ron's father could do.

"How about you?" I asked.

He shook his head. "I'm no strong man, Harry George," he said. I put the phone book away. He could at least have tried.

Then I remembered how once my mom and I had watched my dad climb a tall ladder, crawl up the roof, hang onto a chimney, and reach way out to rescue my kitten. We were scared my dad would fall. Maybe my dad isn't real strong, but he sure is brave. So I told Ron all about what my dad had done.

"Aw, that's nothing, Harry George," Ron said. He was not impressed. "My father fought in the war. He has a whole box full of medals he won for bravery."

After school, I watched my dad fix my bike. I looked at all the tools in his box. I wished they were medals.

"How come you never fought in the war?" I casually asked my dad.

"Flat feet and poor eyesight," my dad said. "They couldn't use me. I was lucky."

"Lucky?" I exclaimed. "You could've won a lot of medals, like Ron's father."

"Ron's father?" my dad said. "Oh, I remember him. The fellow who tears up telephone books. So he won medals, did he?"

"For bravery," I explained.

"Well, good for him," said my dad, and he shut his tool box with a bang.

Later, my dad and I finished the model plane we had been working on. I could hardly wait to show it to Ron.

"See what my dad and I made?" I said to him. "I bet you and your father never made anything like this."

"Aw, that's nothing, Harry George," Ron answered. "My father doesn't fool around with model planes. He flies real ones instead. The kind that take off and land on a carrier. That's dangerous stuff!"

As soon as I got home, I asked my dad if he would like to be a pilot.

"I don't care that much about flying," he told me.

"Why not?" I asked.

"Well, let's just say I feel better getting off a plane than I do getting on."

I wished he hadn't said that. I started to walk away.

"Wait a minute," said my dad. "Does Ron's father happen to be an airline pilot?"

"Oh no," I replied. "He flies fighter jets on carriers for the Navy."

"That figures," I heard my dad mutter.

The next evening, there was an open house at school. I went with my mom and dad. They looked at my work and talked to my teacher.

"Is Ron's father here?" my dad casually asked her. "Harry George is really impressed with him. I'd like to meet him."

My teacher looked at me in surprise.

"You must be thinking of someone else," she said. "Ron's father died years ago."

I walked home like a robot. I couldn't talk or think. "How could Ron do that to me?" I asked. "We were friends. Why did he have to lie to me?"

"Maybe it didn't seem like lying to Ron," my dad said.

"All that junk about tearing the telephone book," I said, "and the medals, and flying a plane. All lies! I believed him. I can never be friends with him again. Never!"

I turned my back and walked out of the kitchen. I wondered what it would be like to have a make-believe father instead of a real dad like mine. I'm glad my dad is real.

The next morning I told my dad that maybe I'd be friends with Ron after all. That's how the three of us began doing things together.

At recess today, I heard Ron say to some kids, "Harry George's father takes us fishing. He knows ten different ways to make paper airplanes. Harry George's father is really something."

Yes, that's my dad, all right. He is really something!

1. What did Harry George learn about his dad?

2. Why did Ron brag about his father?

3. Whom did Ron brag about at the end of the story?

4. Did your feelings about Ron change as you read the story? Why?

5. When did you know that Harry George thought his dad was "really something"?

When we read a story, we learn about the characters. Below are characteristics of Ron's dad and Harry George's dad. Decide which man each characteristic is describing.

1. has flat feet and poor eyesight

2. tears up telephone books

3. flies real fighter jets

4. doesn't care for flying

5. won a lot of medals

Prewrite

Think about the characteristics of the two dads described in "My Dad Is Really Something." How are Harry George's dad and the man Ron described as his dad the same? How are the two dads different?

Compose

Choose one of the activities below.

1. Write a paragraph that describes Harry George's dad as Harry George knows him.

2. Write a paragraph that describes Ron's dad as Ron wanted him to be.

Revise

Check your work carefully to make sure you have written a clear description. If necessary, add more detailed sentences to make your paragraph interesting.

Thinking About "Portholes"

People's views can change, and the people in this unit are proof of that. You walked along the shore with Elisabeth and saw how she learned that the beach holds many different kinds of treasures. You looked through a telescope with Galileo and saw how he could change the way people thought about Earth and the other planets. You heard Harry George try to change his dad until he realized how lucky he was to have a dad.

In some of the stories you read, the author wanted to give information. Which stories were written to inform? In other stories, the author wanted to make you laugh. Which stories were written to entertain?

As you read other stories, watch the characters closely. Watch to see if the characters are the same at the end of the story as they seemed to be in the beginning.

1. The theme of "Portholes" is that people's views can change. Which characters learned that a person can change things by the way he or she treats others? Which character changed people's ideas by what he or she learned about the world?

2. Name one story that could happen and one story that could not happen in real life.

3. Name two stories that give facts or information.

4. In two of the stories the characters are in danger. What are the titles of these stories?

5. How are Miss Moody, Jimmy, and Galileo alike?

Read on Your Own

What the Sea Left Behind by Mimi G. Carpenter. Down East. This book is about a girl who lives on the coast of Maine. She and her mother paint pictures of the things they find on the shore.

Beach Bird by Carol Carrick. Dial. This book is about a day in a gull's life. It shows how he searches for food, fights with other birds, and settles down for the night.

Matilda Jane by Roy and Jean Gerrard. David and Charles. This book is about a child's visit to the English seashore in the early 1900's. She sees many things, including a brass band and tramcars.

The Beachcomber's Book by Bernice Kohn. Puffin. This book describes many different things found on the beach. It also explains how to collect them and use them for crafts and cooking.

Time of Wonder by Robert McCloskey. Viking. This book is about what it is like to live on an island in Maine. It shows children fishing, boating, playing on the beach, and experiencing a hurricane.

A New True Book: Animals of the Sea and Shore by Illa Podendorf. Childrens Press. This book is about creatures that live in the sea and on the seashore. It includes many different animals, with fur or shells, fins or legs, spiny skins or soft bodies.

Posy by Charlotte Pomerantz. Greenwillow. Posy and her father talk about things she used to do when she was a little girl.

Beach Party by Joanne Ryder. Warne. Rose's family spends a fun day at the beach on her uncle's birthday.

Discovering the Stars by Laurence Santrey. Troll. This book describes different kinds of stars. It also tells about constellations and about how stars were used in the past and how they are used today.

Rachel and Obadiah by Brinton Turkle. Dutton. Two children plan a race to carry the news of the next ship's arrival in Nantucket.

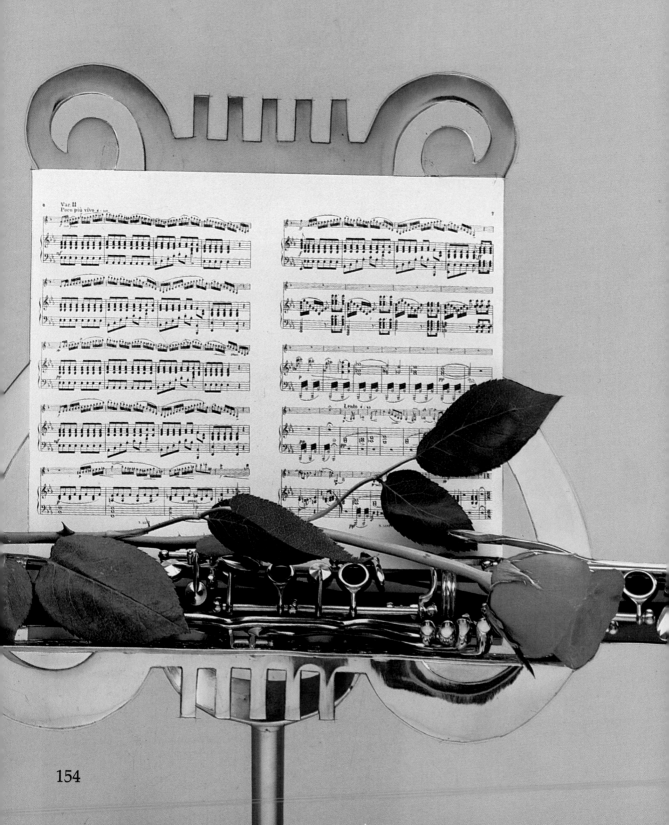

Unit 3
Beauty

Have you ever thought about the kinds of beauty that surround you? There is beauty found in nature. An artist creates beauty with brushes and paint. Think about how musicians and writers create beautiful sounds and stories. They express themselves through their work.

The characters in this unit invite you to join them as they add beauty to their worlds. Come! Roam the countryside and see how easy it is to make the land more beautiful. How do you think listening to music can add to the beauty that surrounds you?

As you read, think about how the characters try to make the world a better place. Turn the page and enter a world of beauty.

A Wizard tries to make the world more beautiful. How does he do this?

The Great Blueness

story and pictures by Arnold Lobel

Long ago there were no colors in the world at all. Almost everything was gray, and what was not gray was black or white. It was a time that was called The Great Grayness.

Every morning a Wizard who lived during the time of The Great Grayness would open his window to look out at the wide land.

"Something is very wrong with the world," he would say. "It is hard to tell when the rainy days stop and the sunny days begin."

The Wizard would often go down the stairs to his dark, gray cellar. There, just to amuse himself and to forget about the drab world outside, he would make wonderful magic potions and spells.

One day while the Wizard was mixing and stirring a little of this and a bit of that, he saw something strange in the bottom of his pot.

"What good-looking stuff I have made!" he exclaimed. "I will make some more right away."

"What is it?" asked the neighbors when they saw the Wizard painting his house.

"A color," said the Wizard. "I call it *blue*."

"Please," cried the neighbors, "please give us some!"

"Of course," said the Wizard.

And that was how The Great Blueness came to be. After a short time everything in the world was blue. Trees were blue. Bees were blue. Wheels and evening meals were blue. The Wizard would pedal out on his blue bicycle to look around at the wide, blue world. He would say, "What a perfect day we are having."

But The Blueness was not so perfect. After a long time all that blue made everyone sad. Children played no games. They sulked in their blue backyards. Mothers and fathers sat at home and stared gloomily at the blue pictures on the walls of their blue living rooms.

"This Blueness is too depressing," said the neighbors to the Wizard, who was unhappier than anyone.

"Nobody laughs anymore," he said. "Even I myself have not smiled for days. I must do something," said the Wizard as he slouched down the stairs to his dark, blue cellar. There he began to mix and stir a little of this and a bit of that. Soon he saw something new in the bottom of his pot.

"Now here is happier stuff," said the Wizard. "I will make some more right away."

"What is that?" asked the neighbors when they saw the Wizard painting his fence.

"I am calling it *yellow*," said the Wizard.

"May we have some?" begged the neighbors.

"You may," replied the Wizard.

And that was how The Great Yellowness came to be. After a short time everything in the world was yellow. There was not a flyspeck of blue anywhere to be seen. Pigs were yellow. Wigs were yellow. Stairs and dentist chairs were yellow. The Wizard would gallop out on his yellow horse to explore the wide, yellow world. He would say, "What a fine day we are having."

But The Yellowness was not so fine. After a long time all that yellow began to hurt everyone's eyes. People walked about bumping and thumping into each other. They were squinting and could not see where they were going.

"This Yellowness is too bright and blinding," said the neighbors to the Wizard.

"You don't have to tell me," moaned the Wizard, who had a cold towel on his head. "Everyone has a headache, and so do I."

So the Wizard stumbled down the stairs to his dark, yellow cellar. There he mixed and stirred a little of this and a bit of that. Soon he saw something different in the bottom of his pot.

"This is handsome stuff," declared the Wizard. "I will make some more right away."

"What do you call that?" asked the neighbors when they saw the Wizard painting his flowers.

"*Red*," answered the Wizard.

"We would like some too," pleaded the neighbors.

"Right away," said the Wizard.

That was how The Great Redness came to be. After a short time everything in the world was red. Mountains were red. Fountains were red. Cheese and afternoon teas were red. The Wizard would sail out in his red boat to see what he could see of the wide, red world. He would say, "What a glorious day we are having."

But The Redness was not so glorious. After a long time all that red put everyone into a very bad temper. Children spent their days fighting and punching each other while mothers and fathers argued loudly. A furious crowd of neighbors marched to the Wizard's house.

"This awful Redness is all your fault," they shouted.

The Wizard stormed down the stairs to his dark, red cellar. He mixed and stirred for many days. He used all the magic that he could think of to find a new color, but all that he made was more blue, more yellow, and more red. The Wizard worked until all of his pots were filled to the top.

The pots were so full that they soon overflowed. The blue and the yellow and the red all began to mix together. It was a terrible mess. But when the Wizard saw what was happening, he exclaimed, "That is the answer!" And he danced joyfully around the cellar.

The Wizard mixed the red with the blue and made a new color. Then he mixed the yellow with the blue and made a new color. The Wizard mixed the yellow with the red and made a new color.

"Hurrah!" he shouted, and he mixed the red and the blue and the yellow in all kinds of different ways.

"Look at these beautiful things I have made!" said the Wizard when he was finished.

"What are they?" asked the neighbors.

"I call them purple and green and orange and brown," said the Wizard.

"They are a sight for sore eyes," cried the neighbors, "but which one shall we choose this time?"

"You must take them all," said the Wizard.

The people did take all the colors the Wizard had made. After a short time they found good places for each one. And after a long time when the Wizard opened his window, he would look out and say, "What a perfectly fine and glorious day we are having!"

The neighbors brought the Wizard gifts of red apples and green leaves and yellow bananas and purple grapes and blue flowers. At last the world was too beautiful ever to be changed again.

Discuss the Selection

1. How did the Wizard make the world more beautiful?

2. What happened when everything in the world was painted blue? Yellow? Red?

3. How did the Wizard solve these problems about color?

4. Would you choose a blue, yellow, or red world to live in? Why?

5. When did you know the world would soon be colorful?

Apply the Skills

Change a detail word in each sentence below. Give other words that you could use in place of the underlined word. The first one is done.

1. After a <u>short</u> time everything was blue.
   long *or* little

2. Now here is <u>happier</u> stuff.

3. What a <u>fine</u> day we are having!

164

Think and Write

Prewrite

Look around you. Where do you see color? Think about how color makes the world more beautiful. What would the world be like without color?

Compose

Choose one of the activities below.

1. Write a paragraph that tells what your favorite color is. Tell how this color makes you feel, and describe at least three things that are this color.

2. Write a poem about color. You may wish to tell about only one color or to tell about several colors in your poem. Be sure to give your poem a title.

Revise

Check your work. Be sure you have followed the directions given in the activity you have chosen. If changes are needed, make them.

The Colors Live

by Mary O'Neill

The Colors live
Between black and white
In a land that we
Know best by sight.
But knowing best
Isn't everything,
For colors dance
And colors sing,
And colors laugh
And colors cry—
Turn off the light
And colors die,
And they make you feel
Every feeling there is
From the grumpiest grump
To the fizziest fizz.
And you and you and I
Know well
Each has a taste
And each has a smell
And each has a wonderful
Story to tell. . . .

Colorful Language

Just as an artist uses paint to create a picture on a canvas, a writer uses words to create a picture on a page. Read this description of a scene:

It was a cold, stormy day. The sky was full of clouds. The raindrops hit the ground.

Now read another description of the same scene. This time, the writer has used special words to make you hear and feel the rain.

It was a cold, stormy day. The sky was full of clouds. *Plop, plop. Plip, plip. Splash, splish* went the raindrops as they hit the ground.

The writer has used the words *plop, plip, splash,* and *splish* to imitate the sounds that rain makes when it hits the ground. These words make the scene seem more alive and interesting.

Now read paragraphs **A** and **B**. Decide which paragraph helps you see and hear what is happening.

A

The artist entered the room. She dropped the case she used to carry her paints. All the jars of paint broke and spilled out over the floor. The wind blew the door shut behind her.

B

Thump! The artist entered the room. Bang! She dropped the case she used to carry her paints. Crash! Splat! All the jars of paint broke and spilled out over the floor. Whoosh! The wind blew the door shut behind her.

Which paragraph did you think was more interesting? What words did the writer use to help you hear sounds? In paragraph **B**, the writer uses the words *click, bang, crash, splat,* and *whoosh* to help you see and hear what is happening.

As you read, look for the words that writers use to help you see and hear sounds. When you write, try to think of words to use that will help your writing come alive for the reader.

How can a one-man band bring beauty to a town? What does the author do to make the story come alive?

Ty's One-man Band

by Mildred Pitts Walter

The sun rose aflame. It quickly dried the dew and baked the town. Another hot, humdrum day. Ty's mother was washing clothes, and his father was busy unloading feed for the chickens. His sister was in the kitchen. Ty had nothing fun to do.

Ty thought of the tall cool grass at the pond and decided to go there.

At the pond, big trees sank their roots down deep and lifted their branches up, up, toward the sky. The grass grew tall enough to hide a boy as big as Ty. He lay quiet, listening. Step-th-hump . . . Ty pressed his ear to the ground. He heard it again: step-th-hump, step-th-hump, step-th-hump. What could it be? Step-th-hump, step-th-hump, closer it came. Then Ty saw a man with only one leg. The other leg was a wooden peg.

The man walked to the water's edge and set a bundle down. He took out a tin cup, a tin plate, a

spoon, and some food. After he ate, he washed his
dishes in the pond. Then the man tossed the cup,
plate, and spoon in the air one after the other, over
and over and over and caught them all. "He's a jug-
gler!" Ty thought. Then the man beat a rhythm with
the spoon on the cup: tink-ki-tink-ki-ki-tink-ki-tink;
and on the plate: tank-ka-tank-ka-ka-tank-ka-tank;
and then on the cup and plate: tink-ki-tink-ki-tank.

"He's a drummer, too," Ty said to himself. Ty
walked closer to the man. Ty felt his heart beat:
thump, thump.

"Who are you?" Ty asked suddenly.

"My name is Andro. I'm a one-man band," said the man, "and I'm at your service."

"What's a one-man band?" asked Ty.

"I'll show you. Go home and get a washboard and two wooden spoons, a tin pail and a comb. I'll come into town at sundown and make music for you and your friends."

Ty hurried home. A one-man band! Could he remember all those things to get? Wooden spoons, a tin pail, a washboard . . . there was something else. What had he forgotten? Ty tried to think. He scratched his head. A comb!

"Wait until I tell my friends," he thought. "They'll come and hear the music, too."

At home Ty ran to his brother Jason's room.

"May I use your comb for the one-man band?"

"For the what?" Ty told Jason about the man who was a band.

"But may I use your comb?"

"Yes, but combs are made for combing hair, not for making music," answered Jason.

Ty rushed to the kitchen. His sister was making corn bread. He told her about the man who was a band. "May I use two wooden spoons?"

"Yes," his sister said, "but I never heard them make music." She laughed as Ty rushed off.

He found his mother in the yard, taking in clothes. He told her about Andro. She shook her head. Then she said, "You may use my washboard at sundown. But that board is made for washing, not for making music."

His father was in the shed, putting corn in the pail to feed the chickens. "Of course, you may use the pail, son. But don't bet on hearing a one-man band. Pails are for carrying, not for making music."

Ty gathered together everything Andro had asked for. Then he ran to tell his friends.

The sun turned into a glowing red ball. It sank lower and lower, but the town didn't cool. People fanned themselves on their porches. It was so hot they didn't even talk.

Ty sat under a street lamp in the town square. He waited. Would Andro come? And if he came, what kind of music would he make with Jason's comb, the old washboard, two wooden spoons, and a pail?

Then in the darkness he heard a step-th-hump, step-th-hump, step-th-hump. Andro was coming!

"I'm here at your service," said Andro. Andro looked at all the things. He turned them about one by one. "These will make fine music," he said as he sat with his good leg folded under him. He placed the spoons between his fingers, and he moved them very fast. Quack-quack-quacket-t-quack. The empty square filled with the sound of ducks.

Then Andro made the sound of horses dancing slowly, Clip-clop-clip-clop-clop. They danced faster, clipty-clop, clipty-clop, clipty-clop-clop. Faster still, cl-oo-py, cl-oo-pop, cl-oo-pop-pop-pop-pop-pop. "Hi ho, Silver!" Andro shouted.

Ty clapped and clapped. Andro took a thin piece of tissue paper from his pocket. Carefully he folded the tissue paper over the comb. Before Ty could ask what that was all about, Andro was making music.

One by one people began to leave their porches. They pressed in closer and clapped their hands and tapped their feet in rhythm as Andro played and danced to his own music. His peg leg went tap-tap-ti-ti-tappity-tap, tappity-tap-tap-ti-ti-tap. He twirled, skipped, and danced 'round and 'round in the spotlight of the street lamp.

Andro stopped dancing and began to make sounds
on the washboard. As he passed his fingers over the
board, Andro made many sounds that Ty thought
sounded very real. Ty could hear water falling, rush-
ing down a hill over rocks, then gurgling in a stream,
and then trickling to a drip, like from a faucet. Best
of all were sounds of a big freight train puffing
slowly, then faster, faster, faster still, then passing
by with the whistle far away.

"More! More! More!" the people shouted.

Andro set the pail down. With a spoon in his hand, he hit the pail, his wooden leg, and the other spoon. Di-de-le-dum, di-de-le-dum, de-di-la-di-ti-do, de-di-la-de-ti-do, chuck-chick-chu-dum, chuck-chick-chu-dum.

Boys and girls, mothers and fathers, even the babies clapped their hands. Some danced and twirled in the street. Whenever the music stopped, everybody shouted, "More!"

Andro let Ty take turns using the instruments. Ty's friends wanted turns, too. Soon they played together like a one-man band. Everybody danced. Only Ty saw Andro slip away back into the night.

1. How does the author make this story come alive?

2. Why was it good for the town when Andro came?

3. Why did Ty gather all the things that Andro asked him to get?

4. What did you think when Andro slipped away unseen into the night?

5. When did you know that Andro had changed the town?

Sometimes authors use words to imitate sounds. Tell what words you might use to imitate the following sounds.

1. water dripping off the roof, one drop at a time

2. wheels of an old-time train going down the track

3. a bee flying around

Prewrite

How did Andro use ordinary things to make music? Study the list of words below. Decide what the words sound like. The first one is done for you.

quack-quack—ducks   ka-boom

rat-a-tat-tat   swoosh

Compose

Choose one of the activities below.

1. Write a paragraph about something that has happened to you. Use words that imitate sounds to make your story more interesting.

2. Write a paragraph that tells how Andro used ordinary things like a comb to make music. Then write one sentence about something ordinary that you could use to make music.

Revise

Read your paragraph or story. If changes are needed, make them.

Follow Directions
Make Musical Instruments

Ty and his friends made simple musical instruments from pots, pails, a washboard, a comb, and other household items. By following directions, you can learn how to make some simple musical instruments. Then you can have your own class band.

Here are some important things to keep in mind when following written directions:

- Be sure to read all the steps very carefully. Then read them again. Make sure you understand what you are to do.
- Gather together the things you will need.
- Begin with step 1 of the directions and follow all the steps in order. Be sure not to leave out any of the steps.

A kazoo is one simple instrument that you can make.

Things you will need:
wax paper
scissors
a 5-inch, or 12-cm, cardboard tube
a rubber band

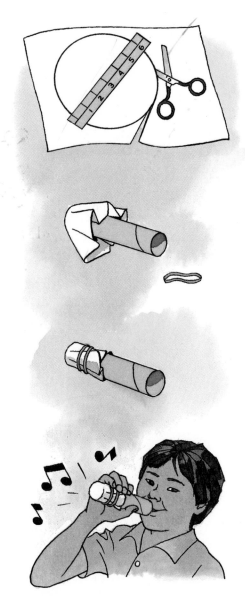

1. Cut out about a 6-inch, or 15-cm, circle of wax paper.

2. Put the wax paper over one end of the tube.

3. Wrap the rubber band tightly around the wax paper to hold it in place on the tube.

4. Hum a tune into the open end of the tube. The kazoo will change your voice to make a buzzing sound.

Now follow these directions to make a comb harmonica.

Things you will need:
scissors
a small, clean comb
a piece of wax paper or tissue paper

1. Cut the wax paper or tissue paper so that it is the same length as the comb. Make sure the paper is wide enough to cover both sides of the teeth of the comb.

2. Hold the comb so the teeth are pointing up.

3. Fold the wax paper or tissue paper over the top of the teeth.

4. Hold the wax paper or tissue paper on the comb at both ends.

5. Put your mouth against one side of the paper-covered comb and hum into the comb.

Here are directions for making a rubber-band guitar.

Things you will need:

    empty tissue box

    four or five rubber bands

    two 6-inch, or 15-cm, wooden dowels or

    two unsharpened pencils

1. Put the rubber bands around the tissue box and across the opening.

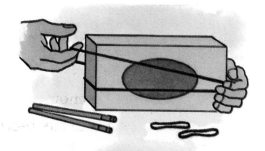

2. Put the pencils under the rubber bands on either side of the opening in the tissue box.

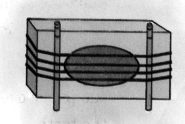

3. Now try playing your guitar by plucking the rubber band strings.

Now you have made three simple instruments. Try playing them with other members of your class.

Beauty means different things to different people. What does beauty mean to the Queen? What does the Mirror have to say about beauty?

Snow White and Friends

by Val R. Cheatham

CHARACTERS:

Narrator   Woodsman

Queen   Doc

Snow White   Dopey

Mirror

SCENE 1

Setting: The Queen's throne room. Mirror is placed near throne. The Narrator enters and speaks.

Narrator: This play is about a little girl who grew up and became beautiful. Her name is Snow White. As the scene opens, we see the wicked Queen. (*Queen enters.*)

Adapted from *Skits and Spoofs for Young Actors* by Val R. Cheatham. Copyright © 1977 by Val R. Cheatham. Published by Plays, Inc., Boston, MA. This play is for reading purposes only. For permission to perform, write to Plays, Inc., 120 Boylston Street, Boston, MA 02116. Reprinted by permission of Plays, Inc.

Queen: Tell me, Mirror, am I still the most lovely creature that ever lived?

Mirror: To hear the things I have to say, you must ask the proper way.

Queen: Oh, you and your rhymes!

Mirror: A looking glass is all I can be, when you forget to question me.

Queen: Oh, all right! All right! Who's the fairest of them all?

Mirror: There are some things, O my Queen, of which I joke a lot, but where your beauty is concerned, you know I kid you not! A lovely sight—young Snow White.

Queen: Snow White? I can't have this. For someone to be lovelier than I is out of the question. She must be done away with. I'll call the Woodsman!

Woodsman: *(entering)* You called?

Queen: Yes. I have a little job for you.

Woodsman: Chopping down trees?

Queen: Well, it's a kind of chopping.

Woodsman: Name it, my Queen. It shall be done.

Queen: You see, there's this girl, Snow White. She's more beautiful than I. Snow White must die because there can never be anyone else alive to equal my beauty.

Woodsman: You know getting rid of the girl is not my line of work.

Queen: You have a choice between two heads.

Woodsman: Two? One is enough!

Queen: A choice between two, Woodsman. Yours or the girl's. . . . Well?

Woodsman: Very well, my Queen. When you put it that way . . .

Queen: *(to Mirror)* Heh, heh, heh. How about that, Mirror-Mirror-on-the-wall?

SCENE 2

Setting: The forest.

Narrator: What will happen to young Snow White? In this scene, the Woodsman and Snow White are in the forest. (*Woodsman and Snow White enter; Narrator exits.*)

Woodsman: This, Snow White, is a pine tree.

Snow White: Oh! How very interesting.

Woodsman: Now, can you see what's over there?

Snow White: (*bending over and looking off*) Where?

Woodsman: (*prepares ax, then drops it on the ground*) I can't do it!

Snow White: Can't do what, Mr. Woodsman?

Woodsman: I can't obey the Queen. She sent me out here to get rid of you because of your beauty.

Snow White: Me? Why, only yesterday they were calling me the Ugly Duckling.

Woodsman: That was yesterday. You stay here, and I'll go tell the Queen you're dead.

Snow White: I'm concerned. Will that be safe for you, Mr. Woodsman?

Woodsman: I'll be all right. The Queen's getting old. Many girls are more beautiful than she is. Soon you will be able to go back. I must leave; be careful. *(Woodsman exits.)*

Snow White: Thank you and good-bye. Now, which way shall I go? *(looking off to the right)*

Doc and Dopey: *(enter)* Hi-ho, hi-ho . . .

Snow White: Oh, who are you?

Dopey: We're The Dwarfs.

Snow White: I'm supposed to meet The Seven Dwarfs, and they will take me home and help me.

Doc: That's our name: "The Seven Dwarfs—Littlest Band with the Biggest Beat." He's Dopey, and I'm Doc. Who are you?

Snow White: I'm Snow White. The wicked Queen wants me done away with because of my beauty.

Doc: Can you play drums?

Snow White: No. *(crying)* Oh, why does the Queen hate me so?

Dopey: The Queen doesn't like us either.

Doc: The Dwarfs had three hits on the top ten. We were getting to be more popular than the Queen, but she fixed that. She sent us to the woods. Now we only play for the sparrows and the blue jays.

Dopey: She said our music was for the birds.

Doc: Are you sure you're not a drummer?

Snow White: I'm really sure. But I can sing.

Doc: That's it! A singer! That could give our sound some real class. *(They exit.)*

189

SCENE 3

Setting: The Queen's throne room.

Narrator: For the next scene we go back to visit the Queen and her magic mirror. Will Snow White stay in the forest and sing with The Dwarfs? Will the Woodsman escape to the woods and become the new drummer for The Dwarfs? (*Mirror is on stage; Queen enters; Narrator exits.*)

Queen: (*looking into the mirror*) There can never be anyone with beauty equal to mine. Isn't that right, Mirror?

Mirror: To hear the things I have to say, you must ask the proper way.

Queen: All right, all right. I'll ask in rhyme. Mirror-Mirror-on-the-wall-who's-the-fairest-of-them-all? Now, hurry up and tell me.

Mirror: Raven hair as soft as silk, eyes so bright and blue, blushing sunshine in her cheeks, a heart so kind and true—

Queen: Wait a minute! Raven hair? You're not going to give me that Snow White speech again, are you? Remember? The Woodsman?

Mirror: Very much alive is Snow White, our lovely heroine. The tenderhearted Woodsman was too kind to do her in. She's taken cover with some dwarfs, who helped her in her flight. Now she's singing happy tunes with the little band each night.

Queen: Snow White is still alive! What's a queen to do when no one will obey her?

Mirror: Beauty is not meant to be one's only goal in life. It's courage, faith, and goodness that can help one get through life. These things will stay right with you; they can't be bought or sold. Beauty changes with the years, and, face it, Queen—you're old.

Queen: I must do something. I'll get rid of Snow White myself. I'll poison her. I'll take this nice, red, juicy *(pulls banana from pocket)* banana? Well, one thing will work as well as another. How about that, Mirror-Mirror-on-the-wall?

SCENE 4

Setting: The forest.

Narrator: As this scene opens, the Queen has brought the poisoned banana to give to Snow White. (*Queen enters; Narrator exits.*)

Queen: Oh, Snow White—where are you? Yoo-hoo! (*Snow White enters.*)

Snow White: Were you calling me?

Queen: Yes. You're such a cute little thing and do such a good job singing with the band, I want you to have this banana.

Snow White: You've heard my singing?

Queen: Yes, I've heard you. I used to do some singing myself. Here, have a banana.

Snow White: I really don't care for this banana.

Queen: But it's such a beauty, and I do want you to have it.

Snow White: All right, but I don't like bananas.

Queen: This one is . . . different. (*Snow White peels it and takes a bite; then she drops to floor.*) Let's hear you sing now! (*moves away from Snow White*)

Queen: *(Doc and Dopey enter.)* Hello, who are you?

Doc: Doc Dwarf, leader of The Seven Dwarfs. Would you like to come hear us play? *(takes apple from pocket)* Have an apple.

Queen: Thank you. *(Queen eats apple as she and Doc exit.)*

Dopey: *(turns and sees Snow White on the floor)* What's wrong with Snow White?

Woodsman: *(enters)* She is waiting for me! The Queen just gave her a poisoned banana, and I'm the Prince with the cure that will get our heroine back on her feet. Let's see—*(searches pockets, finds bottle)* Banana-cure! *(passes bottle under Snow White's nose)*

Snow White: *(sitting up and rubbing eyes)* You're the Woodsman.

Woodsman: Wrong! I am the Prince dressed as a tenderhearted Woodsman to escape from the Queen. But that's all ended now. Doc just gave her a Boy Scout Apple. One bite and she will act like a true Boy Scout. She will also feel like doing a good deed every day!

1. Why was the Queen such a mean person? What does beauty mean to the Queen?

2. What good things happened to Snow White because the Queen was jealous of her?

3. What happened to the Queen after Doc Dwarf gave her an apple?

4. Whose definition of beauty do you like better, the Queen's or the Mirror's? Why?

5. When did you know that Snow White's problems would be solved?

The characters in "Snow White and Friends" say funny and silly things. For example, the Queen says, "You're not going to give me that Snow White speech again, are you?"

Pick one character: the Queen, the Woodsman, or Dopey. Find two lines this character says that are funny or silly. Be ready to read the lines aloud.

Prewrite

Think about how the play you have just read is like the fairy tale "Snow White and the Seven Dwarfs." What things were changed to make the play different from the fairy tale?

Compose

Choose one of the activities below.

1. Write a paragraph that tells how the play "Snow White and Friends" and the fairy tale "Snow White and the Seven Dwarfs" are alike and how they are different.

2. Think about another fairy tale such as "Cinderella," "Goldilocks and the Three Bears," or "The Emperor's New Clothes." Rewrite one of the fairy tales in your own words. Change the story to make it funny and to make it fit into the present time.

Revise

Check your work. Be sure you have followed the directions given in the activity you have chosen. If changes are needed, make them.

Beauty

by E-Yeh-Shure'

Beauty is seen
In the sunlight,
The trees, the birds,
Corn growing and people working
Or dancing for their harvest.

Beauty is heard
In the night,
Wind sighing, rain falling,
Or a singer chanting
Anything in earnest.

Beauty is in yourself.
Good deeds, happy thoughts
That repeat themselves
In your dreams,
In your work,
And even in your rest.

Topic, Main Idea, and Details

Look at the picture. It shows something happening. What is the picture showing? Yes, the picture is about gardening. "Gardening" is the **topic** of the picture. What is the most important thing the picture shows? *The children are planting a garden.* The **main idea** is that the children are planting a garden. Look to see what each child is doing. One is planting seeds. Another is raking. The last child is watering the garden. These are the details in the picture. All these details together are **supporting details** for the main idea: *the children are planting a garden.*

Just as a picture can have a main idea, many of the paragraphs you read have main ideas, too. Read the paragraph below and find the main idea.

Seed plants grow in many different places. Some plants grow better in places that are hot while others grow better in cold places. Some need a great deal of sunlight; some grow best in shade. Some plants can be found in very wet places, while others may grow in very dry places. Some plants may even grow in water. Look in open fields, in gardens, in the cracks of side-walks, and in flowerpots. You may find seed plants growing there.

What is the main idea? In this paragraph, the first sentence, *Seed plants grow in many different places,* states the main idea.

The main idea, however, will not always be the first sentence of the paragraph. To find the main idea, first look for the topic of the paragraph. The topic is what the paragraph is about. The topic of the paragraph you just read is "seed plants." The main idea is the most important thing the paragraph says about the topic.

Now read the paragraph about seed plants once more. Look for the details that support the main idea.

Did you notice that every sentence tells you something about the different places that seed plants grow? Read the following list. It shows the details from the paragraph that support the main idea: *Seed plants grow in different places.*

1. They may grow in cold or hot places.
2. They may grow in sunlight or shade.
3. They may grow in very wet or very dry places.
4. Some seed plants even grow in water.
5. Seed plants grow in open fields, gardens, cracks of sidewalks, and flowerpots.

Textbook Application: Finding Topic, Main Idea, and Details in Science

A long article with many paragraphs can also have a topic, a main idea, and supporting details. Textbooks and other informational materials are often organized in this way. As you read these kinds of materials, look for the topic, the main idea, and the details. These will help you understand and remember what you are reading.

Read the following paragraphs which are taken from a textbook. The sidenotes will help you find the topic, main idea, and details.

ROOTS

What Do Roots Do?

Did you ever think about what roots do? Have you ever tried to pull out weeds in a garden? Did they come out easily? Weeds and most other seed plants have roots that grow in the ground. In some plants the roots may grow more than six meters (20 feet) deep. Roots hold plants in place. Look at trees during a storm sometime. Even a strong wind usually cannot blow them over.

What else do roots do? Roots take in water and minerals [min′ər·əls] that plants need. Plants need minerals to grow and to be healthy. The water and minerals are carried in tiny tubes in the roots to the stem.

In some plants, food is stored in the roots. Have you ever eaten a carrot, radish, or beet? If so, you have eaten a root with stored food.

—*Silver Burdett Science*, Silver Burdett

"Roots" is the topic of this article.

The main idea of this article is easy to find. It is written below the title.

This sentence gives one supporting detail for the main idea. What other supporting details can you find?

The sidenotes showed the topic, the main idea, and the supporting details in the first paragraph. The other supporting details are listed on the next page.

What Do Roots Do?

1. Roots hold plants in place.
2. Roots take in water and minerals.
3. Roots store food for some plants.

Now read different paragraphs taken from the same science book. As you read, decide what the topic, main idea, and details are.

Stems of Seed Plants

There are four main kinds of seed plants. They are trees, shrubs, herbs, and vines. Each has a different kind of stem.

A **tree** has one main stem called a trunk. The trunk is a woody stem. It is stiff and hard and covered with bark. Maples, oaks, and pines are common types of trees.

A **shrub** is smaller than a tree and has many woody stems. Some shrubs are called bushes. Rosebushes and lilac [lī′lak′] bushes are types of shrubs.

An **herb** is another kind of seed plant. Herbs are small plants with soft rather than woody stems. Many herbs die at the end of one growing season. Grasses, flowers, and most weeds are types of herbs. Goldenrod is a weed that is an herb.

Many different herbs are used as food. Some people even have herb gardens. Parsley [pärs′lē] and chives [chīvz] are two types of herbs.

A **vine** is another kind of plant with a soft stem. Vines cannot stand by themselves. They climb by wrapping around other things, or they creep along the ground. Cucumber, pumpkin, and ivy are vines.

—*Silver Burdett Science*, Silver Burdett

What is the topic of the selection? What is the main idea? The topic is "Stems." The main idea is that seed plants have four kinds of stems. Can you find the supporting details for the main idea? Read the article again and look for the supporting details. Then, on a separate piece of paper, write the supporting details in a list.

As you read textbooks and other informational materials, remember to look for the topic, main idea, and supporting details.

Beauty can be seen in nature. What are several ways that nature spreads its beauty?

Floaters, Poppers, and Parachutes

by Cynthia Overbeck Bix

Have you ever picked up a "wing" on the sidewalk under a maple tree and let it go spinning away on the wind? Or have you ever blown on a dandelion head and watched the white puffs float off like little parachutes? What about burrs? Have you ever picked one off your sock or some other piece of clothing?

If so, you have helped a seed find a new place to grow. The wing, the parachute, and the burr are parts of plants that carry seeds. Inside each seed are all the things needed to grow a new plant.

From spring to autumn, the air and water are filled with these tiny travelers. Dry maple tree wings grow from small flowers. The flowers are on the maple tree in the spring. Each flower grows double wings with one seed in each wing. When the wings are ready to fall, they break apart and come spinning down from the tree. The wings have a good chance of being caught by the wind and carried away. If one of them lands in good soil, the seed inside it may sprout into a tree.

Dandelions also ride the wind. The yellow flower petals die and hundreds of tiny seeds are left on the white head of the dandelion. Each seed has silky hairs on top. When the wind catches these silky hairs, they float like little parachutes. When the silky hairs finally touch down, they may be far away from where they started. They leave their seeds in someone's yard, or in a field. The next spring, dandelions will be found growing where they had not grown before.

Many wind travelers can also float on water because they are so light. The dandelion parachute or the maple wing may be carried by the wind and later be dropped into a stream.

Other travelers can move only by floating on water. The coconut has a hard shell as big as a football, with a large seed inside. It can float because it has lots of air spaces inside. When a ripe coconut falls from a tree onto the beach, the ocean currents may carry it very far away. If the coconut is washed ashore on another beach, it may put down roots and grow into a coconut tree.

Many of the coconut trees that today line the beaches of the tropical Hawaiian Islands grew from coconuts that were washed ashore. The islands had no coconut trees or other plants when they were first formed. Most of the plants that now grow there were brought by water or wind from tropical beaches far away.

with many seeds is left. The ball is covered with very small spines. Each spine is bent at the end like a tiny fishhook and sticks to most things. When a passer-by brushes against a burdock plant, the hooks catch onto clothes or fur and stay there. The seeds fall out of the burr as it is carried along. Many of the seeds will take root in the ground, often far from the place where they were picked up.

Seeds fly and float. Some also hitchhike by catching free rides on the hair of dogs or wild animals, or on somebody's sock or pant leg. Many have hooks, barbs, or spines that stick to things.

One hitchhiking seed carrier that is easy to find is the burr. The burr comes from the burdock, a weed that grows almost any-where. When the burdock's flower dies, a dark-colored ball

Flying, floating, hitchhiking, and popping seeds are always on the move. Many accidents may happen to them. They may be eaten by insects and animals. They may land on poor soil or on no soil at all. Still, enough seeds live for many new plants to grow.

The next time you take a walk, watch for the seeds of the many trees and plants around you. Once you begin to look, you will see the tiny travelers in the air, on the water—everywhere.

Some seeds travel in a surprising way. They pop! The wild touch-me-not is a plant that spreads its seeds by popping. In the summer it has bright orange, yellow, or red flowers. Green pods grow from the flowers. Each pod has five parts with rows of seeds inside. When the pods have grown to their full length, the five parts suddenly curl up and pop. The seeds shoot out in many directions. They may travel as far as 2 yards, or 1.8 meters, away from the plant.

1. Why do most seeds have wings, hairs, burrs, or pods?

2. How do seeds get to new places?

3. Why don't all seeds take root and grow?

4. Of all the ways that seeds travel, which do you think is the most interesting? Why?

5. When did you know why the author chose the title "Floaters, Poppers, and Parachutes"?

Apply the Skills

The main idea of a paragraph or selection is the most important idea. Supporting details tell more about the main idea.

One main idea in "Floaters, Poppers, and Parachutes" is *The wind helps some seeds find a new place to grow.* What is one detail?

Another main idea is *Other travelers can move only by floating on water.* Find two details that support this main idea.

Prewrite

Think about "Floaters, Poppers, and Parachutes." What is the topic of this selection? Find one main idea. What details does the author use to support that main idea?

Compose

Choose one of the activities below.

1. Choose a paragraph from the selection, and list the topic of the paragraph, the main idea, and at least two supporting details.

2. Pretend that you are one of the seeds described in the selection. Then write a paragraph that describes how you traveled from the plant you grew on to a new place. In your paragraph, answer the following questions: What kind of seed are you? How do you travel? Where did you travel on your way to a new place to grow?

Revise

Check your work. Be sure you have followed the directions.

Who is the Lupine Lady? What does she do to make the world more beautiful?

Miss Rumphius

story and pictures by Barbara Cooney

The Lupine Lady lives in a small house overlooking the sea. In between the rocks around her house grow blue and purple and rose-colored flowers. The Lupine Lady is little and old, but she has not always been that way. I know. She is my great-aunt, and she told me so.

Once upon a time there was a little girl, named Alice, who lived in a city by the sea. From the front steps she could see the masts of tall ships. Many years ago her grandfather had come to America on a large sailing ship. Now he lived in the shop at the bottom of the house making figureheads for the front-ends of ships. He also painted pictures of sailing ships and places across the sea. When he was very busy, Alice helped him by painting the skies.

CARVING AND PAINT

EAGLE

HOTEL

DINING SALOON

25

Wm RUMPH

In the evening Alice sat on her grandfather's knee and listened to his stories of faraway places. When he had finished, Alice would say, "When I grow up, I too will go to faraway places, and when I grow old, I too will live beside the sea."

"That is all very well, little Alice," said her grandfather, "but there is a third thing you must do."

"What is that?" asked Alice.

"You must do something to make the world more beautiful," said her grandfather.

"All right," said Alice. But she did not know what that could be.

In the meantime Alice got up and washed her face and ate breakfast. She went to school and came home and did her homework.

And pretty soon she was grown up.

Then my Great-aunt Alice set out to do the three things she had told her grandfather she was going to do. She left home and went to live in another city far from the sea and the salt air. There she worked in a library, dusting books and keeping them from getting mixed up and helping people find the ones they wanted. Some of the books told her about faraway places.

People called her Miss Rumphius now.

Sometimes she went to the conservatory in the middle of the park. When she stepped inside on a wintry day, the warm air wrapped itself around her, and the sweet smell of the flowers filled her nose. "This is almost like a tropical island," said Miss Rumphius. "But not quite."

So Miss Rumphius went to a real tropical island, where people kept monkeys as pets. She walked on long beaches, picking up beautiful shells.

My great-aunt Miss Alice Rumphius climbed tall mountains where the snow never melted. She went through jungles and across deserts. Finally she came to another island, and there, getting off a camel, she hurt her back.

"Well," said Miss Rumphius, "I have certainly seen faraway places. Maybe it is time to find my place by the sea."

And it was, and she did.

From the porch of her new house Miss Rumphius
watched the sun come up; she watched it cross the sky
and sparkle on the water; and she saw it set in glory in
the evening. She started a little garden among the rocks
that surrounded her house, and she planted a few flower
seeds in the stony ground. Miss Rumphius was *almost*
perfectly happy.

"But there is still one more thing I have to do," she
said. "I have to do something to make the world more
beautiful.

"But what? The world already is pretty nice," she
thought, looking out at the ocean.

The next spring Miss Rumphius was not very well. Her back was bothering her again, and she had to stay in bed most of the time.

The flowers she had planted the summer before had come up and bloomed in spite of the stony ground. She could see them from her bedroom window, blue and purple and rose-colored.

"Lupines," said Miss Rumphius with satisfaction. "I have always loved lupines the best. I wish I could plant more seeds this summer so that I could have still more flowers next year."

She was not able to.

After a hard winter spring came. Miss Rumphius was feeling much better. Now she could take walks again. One afternoon she started to go up and over the hill, where she had not been in a long time.

"I don't believe my eyes!" she cried when she got to the top. For there on the other side of the hill was a large patch of blue and purple and rose-colored lupines!

"It was the wind," she said as she knelt in delight. "It was the wind that brought the seeds from my garden here! And the birds must have helped!"

She hurried home and got out her seed catalogues. She sent off to the very best seed house for five bushels of lupine seed.

All that summer Miss Rumphius, her pockets full of seeds, wandered over fields and headlands, sowing lupines. She scattered seeds along the highways and down the country lanes. She flung handfuls of seeds around the schoolhouse and back of the church. She tossed them into hollows and along stone walls.

Her back didn't bother her anymore at all.

The next spring there were lupines everywhere. Fields and hillsides were covered with blue and purple and rose-colored flowers. They bloomed along the highways and down the lanes. Bright patches lay around the schoolhouse and back of the church. Down in the hollows and along the stone walls grew the beautiful flowers.

Miss Rumphius had done the third, the most difficult thing of all!

My Great-aunt Alice, Miss Rumphius, is very old now. Her hair is very white. Every year there are more and more lupines. Now they call her the Lupine Lady. Sometimes my friends stand with me outside her gate, curious to see the old, old lady who planted the fields of lupines. When she invites them in, they come slowly. They think she is the oldest woman in the world. Often she tells us stories of faraway places.

"When I grow up," I tell her, "I too will go to faraway places and come home to live by the sea."

"That is all very well, little Alice," says my great-aunt, "but there is a third thing you must do."

"What is that?" I ask.

"You must do something to make the world more beautiful."

"All right," I say.

But I do not know yet
        what that can be.

1. How did the Lupine Lady get her name?
2. What were the three things Miss Rumphius wanted to do during her life?
3. How did Miss Rumphius keep her promise to her grandfather?
4. Do you think little Alice will be able to keep her promise to her great-aunt? Why?
5. When did you know what the Lupine Lady did to make the world more beautiful?

Read the sentences below from "Miss Rumphius." Find the words the author used to tell when something happened.

1. After a hard winter, spring came. Miss Rumphius was feeling much better.
2. Before too long, she was grown up.
3. The next spring, there were lupines everywhere.

Prewrite

In the story, Miss Rumphius traveled to many faraway places before she settled in a house by the sea. What do you think she found in those places? Which place do you think would be the most interesting to visit?

Compose

Choose one of the activities below.

1. Pretend that you are Miss Rumphius. Choose one of the faraway places she visited. Write a letter to a friend describing the place you have chosen. Where is it? What does it look like? What have you seen?

2. Imagine that you have just moved into a house by the sea. Write a letter to a friend that tells about living by the sea. Describe the different things you can see.

Revise

Check your work to make sure you have included enough details in your letter. If changes are needed, make them.

Artists add beauty to the world in many ways. How does one popular author and illustrator share beauty with others?

Interview with Barbara Cooney

adapted from an article by Julia Smith

Barbara Cooney is an award-winning author and illustrator of picture books for children. She won the 1983 American Book Award for *Miss Rumphius.*

Barbara Cooney has also won two Caldecott Awards. The Caldecott Award is given each year for the best illustrations in a children's book.

As you read the following interview, you will feel as if you are talking directly to Barbara Cooney. You will learn why this creative author and illustrator decided to work on children's books and what she is like as a person.

QUESTION: Why did you decide to become an illustrator of children's books?

ANSWER: When I was young, I loved reading series books. They went on and on and you didn't have to say good-bye to the characters. Of course I read other books, too—all the time. Books help you create pictures in your mind.

My mother was an artist who loved to paint. She helped me experiment with color. After I finished school, I knew I wanted to paint pictures. I decided that illustrating books for children would let me be the most creative.

QUESTION: Where did you get the idea to write and illustrate *Miss Rumphius*?

ANSWER: My husband and I were building a house in Maine. I asked one of the painters why there were so many lovely flowers growing all around. He told me about Hilda. Hilda is a real-life Lupine Lady who planted the lupines. The story began to grow in my mind, until one day, I sat down and wrote it. I had something in my head and I just had to get it out. *Miss Rumphius* was the result.

QUESTION: Did you put anything from your own life in the illustrations for *Miss Rumphius*?

ANSWER: I put in lots of little details that make me happy. These are my shawl, my favorite armchair, and a picture of my grandson. I don't know if other people notice all these details, but they make me happy.

QUESTION: You have won two Caldecott Awards for your illustrations. What books received those awards?

ANSWER: I won the Caldecott Award in 1959 for the illustrations in *Chanticleer and the Fox.* Many of my early illustrations were of animals. People will give you little furry animal stories if you draw good fur.

Then, in 1980, I won a second Caldecott Award for *Ox-Cart Man.* I spent most of my life in New England. That is why I was able to show a farmer and his family and the busy marketplace in that book.

QUESTION: How do you begin to illustrate a book?

ANSWER: When I begin to illustrate a book, I start with page one. Books are like movies. One's eye moves from frame to frame in a sequence. I must keep that sequence in mind to keep the reader's eye always interested.

First, I make what is called a dummy of the book. It is a rough, messy copy of what the book will be like. Then, I begin the final illustrations, working carefully to get just the right colors, and just the perfect tone. The book jacket comes last. The book jacket is like the label on a can of tomatoes. You can't put a tomato on the label until you know you have a tomato in the can.

QUESTION: What other things do you like to do besides work on children's books?

ANSWER: I also love to garden, cook, photograph, travel the world, and be a grandmother. I love life and plan to live to be one hundred years old!

1. How does the interview with Barbara Cooney tell about the way she shares beauty with others?

2. Why did Barbara Cooney become a children's book illustrator?

3. What awards have Barbara Cooney's books received?

4. Why do you think an interview with Barbara Cooney is in this book?

5. How does the interview help you learn what Barbara Cooney is like as a person?

Some selections are written to entertain, and some are written to give us information. Many selections can do both. "Interview with Barbara Cooney" is enjoyable, yet its purpose is to give us information about Barbara Cooney.

Find three facts about Ms. Cooney that are given in the selection.

Prewrite

How would you use the information from the interview to write an article? What did Barbara Cooney say about how she illustrates a book?

Compose

Choose one of the activities below.

1. Use the information given in the interview about Barbara Cooney to write a factual paragraph. Write a topic sentence for your paragraph and support the main idea with at least three facts about Ms. Cooney.

2. Think about the steps Barbara Cooney takes in illustrating a book. Write a paragraph describing those three steps. Remember to write a sentence that states the main idea.

Revise

Check your work to be sure that you have listed only factual information in your paragraph. Make changes that are needed.

Thinking About "Beauty"

Beauty is all around you. There can be beauty in nature in a blazing sunset, or on a hillside that Miss Rumphius speckled with purple lupines. Music can be beautiful, too. It can be a song you heard or the music Andro made for Ty and his friends.

Think about how some authors used colorful language to help you see and hear their words. How did colorful language make the stories they told more interesting?

What did the Queen learn about the real meaning of beauty? How does Barbara Cooney express her ideas about beauty to her readers? How have the stories taught you that beauty can be found almost everywhere if you look and listen carefully?

The way you look at something helps you decide whether or not it is beautiful. As you read other stories, decide how the characters are helping you find new ways to see beauty.

1. The theme of "Beauty" is that many people add beauty to the world. Which characters in this unit made the world a more beautiful place?

2. In what ways is the world made better in "The Great Blueness," "Ty's One-man Band," "Snow White and Friends," and "Miss Rumphius"?

3. Would you like to hear a band like Ty's or see a field of lupines? Why?

4. Why do you think the Mirror in "Snow White and Friends" tells the truth to the Queen?

5. What is the best expression of beauty that you know? Does anything in these stories compare to it?

Read on Your Own

Ox-Cart Man by Donald Hall. Viking. This beautiful book describes the day-to-day life of an early nineteenth century family throughout the changing seasons. It was illustrated by Barbara Cooney and won the Caldecott Medal for its art work.

Beauty and the Beast by Warwick Hutton. Atheneum. This is a fairy tale about a kind girl whose love releases a prince from a spell. This book has many lovely pictures.

Ben's Trumpet by Rachel Isadora. Greenwillow. Ben wants to be a trumpeter. He only plays an imaginary instrument until someone discovers his dream.

Seeds by Wind and Water by Helene Jordan. Harper. This book describes the many ways that seeds travel. Wind and water, dogs and cats, and even the tires of cars and planes carry seeds from place to place.

SEEDS Pop•Stick•Glide by Patricia Lauber. Crown. This book tells about the many ways that seeds travel and spread.

Geraldine the Music Mouse by Leo Lionni. Pantheon. After a mouse nibbles a large piece of cheese into the shape of a giant mouse with a flute, she hears music for the first time.

Fables by Arnold Lobel. Harper. This book has twenty fables about unusual animals, including one story about an ostrich and a baboon. This book won the Caldecott Medal for its art work.

The Bremen Town Musicians retold by Ilse Plume. Doubleday. This is a lovely retelling of the fairy tale by the Grimm Brothers about three animals who set out to become musicians.

Music, Music for Everyone by Vera B. Williams. Greenwillow. Rosa forms a band with her friends. When they play at many neighborhood events, she is able to earn some money to help her mother and grandmother.

232

Unit 4

Milestones

Long ago, when there were no road signs, large stones were put by the side of the road to mark the miles. That is how the word *milestone* came to be. Today, the word *milestone* is used to mean an important point or a turning point in someone's life.

Imagine what it would be like to live long ago and journey into the wilderness. Think how it would feel to be different from everyone in school. Decide what it would be like to do something that no one else has ever done.

As you read the selections in this unit, you will discover how some of the characters have made a lasting mark on the world in which we live. What milestones did the characters reach?

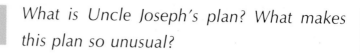

What is Uncle Joseph's plan? What makes this plan so unusual?

Away Goes Sally

by Elizabeth Coatsworth

Sally lived in Old New England with three aunts and two uncles. The family was made up of Aunt Nannie, Aunt Deborah, Aunt Esther, Uncle Joseph, Uncle Eben, and Sally.

After Uncle Joseph received a letter from his cousin in Maine, Uncle Joseph was ready to move the family. He wanted to go to Maine because there were few settlers there. Everyone wanted to move, too, except for his sister Nannie. Aunt Nannie wanted to stay in Massachusetts where they had a nice house and farm. Aunt Nannie told her family that she would never leave her own fire nor sleep in any bed but her own. Uncle Joseph thought of a way to change Aunt Nannie's mind.

As the story begins, Sally and her aunts are returning from a visit to the city of Quincy.

They drove home quickly. When Dorcas, the mare, stopped at the back door it was still light. There was no sign of the uncles or of their hired hand, Jehoshaphat Mountain. Sally started to take the mare to the barn. She was stopped by several voices coming down the road. She heard men's voices, and the screech of heavy runners on snow. The three aunts paused on the doorstep. Sally jumped from the sleigh to watch. Out of the darkness of the last pine trees appeared the strangest thing she had ever seen.

First came Peacock, Uncle Joseph's big horse, with Uncle Joseph on his back. Then came six strong oxen, led by the red pair from their own farm. Beside them

walked Jehoshaphat Mountain and Uncle Eben with long poles. Behind them came a little house on runners. It was a house with windows whose small panes sparkled in the late light. The house had a doorstep, a water-barrel under the drip of the roof, and a chimney pipe from which smoke was rising.

Sally jumped up and down, clapping her mittened hands. Aunt Esther cried in delight. Uncle Joseph waved. Aunt Nannie made no sound.

Slowly the line drew to the step and stopped.

"Nannie," said Uncle Joseph in a serious voice, "here is a house that I built for you and which I give to you with all my heart. Now you may travel to Maine and yet never leave your own fire."

He paused and they all waited. Aunt Nannie's face was blank with surprise and did not show her thoughts. Once she tried to speak but could not. In the long silence Sally heard her own heart pounding like a colt galloping over a frozen meadow.

"Thank you, Brother Joseph," said Aunt Nannie at last in a small gentle voice. "Thank you, my dear. I shall go willingly."

Sally let her breath out in a gasp of joy. Uncle Joseph jumped from the saddle and kissed Aunt Nannie, who cried a little.

"Dorcas will take herself to the barn, Sally," Uncle Joseph called. "Come and see Aunt Nannie's house." They all crowded into the house.

The house was small, of course, but bright with windows. It was warm with the Franklin stove which had a little fire burning in it. Two big beds stood in two corners of the room. They were covered with blue eagle woven quilts. There was a smooth wooden sink and several chairs, and china in racks on the walls. Behind the larger room was a small room with two bunks in it for the uncles.

"There will be sleds for the rest of the furniture, Nannie," went on Uncle Joseph. "I have hired some men and their teams from down the road. You will, I imagine, wish to take our cows. Dorcas and the sleigh will bring up the rear, so that you may all get some air when you grow tired of being in the house. Here, Deborah, are your seeds for a new garden. We will carry some of your bulbs and roots on the sleds."

"How soon do we leave, Brother Joseph?" Aunt Nannie asked as she hung up her cloak on a peg and seated herself in her own chair.

"It's a picture to see you," said Uncle Joseph, smiling at her. They looked at each other and made their peace without a word being spoken. "I wanted this to be a surprise for you like the doll's house I made when you were a little girl. That's why I packed you all off to Quincy to have you out of the way while we furnished the house. You asked when we would leave, Nannie. In a week, if you can be ready, my dear, so that we may have the advantage of the snow. The neighbors will help you.''

"It will be a long trip," went on Uncle Joseph. "When we reach our land, we shall have this house to live in until we can build a better new home, Nannie, on a wider piece of land.''

It was Sally who discovered the six little pots steaming in the rack on the stove. Uncle Eben, always ready to help in any matter of food, showed Sally where a pine table let down from the wall. She found the cloth and silver spoons and the bread. Soon six cups were filled, and they shared their first meal in the house that was to carry them to a new land.

Discuss
the
Selection

1. What was Uncle Joseph's plan?

2. Why was Uncle Joseph's plan so unusual?

3. How did Uncle Joseph get Aunt Nannie to agree to move?

4. Do you think Uncle Joseph's plan was a good idea? Explain your answer.

5. When did you know that Aunt Nannie would not have to leave her fire?

Apply
the
Skills

The *setting* tells about the place and about the time when the story takes place. Below are some ideas from the story. Tell whether these ideas tell mostly about place or time.

1. out of the darkness

2. then came six oxen

3. they all crowded into the house

Prewrite

Sally and her family were going to spend time traveling in a house on runners. Think about how the time in the house on runners might have been different from living in a house that does not move. What might Sally like about living in the house on runners? What things might have been difficult for Sally while they were traveling?

Compose

Choose one of the activities below.

1. Write a paragraph that describes three ways in which Sally's life in the house on runners might have been different from her life in a house that does not move.

2. Pretend that you are Sally. Write a paragraph telling what you liked most about the time you spent traveling in the house on runners.

Revise

Check your work carefully. Be sure you have followed the directions given in the activity you have chosen. If changes are needed, make them.

Old Sturbridge Village is a model of an old village. Read to find out what life was like in early New England.

Old Sturbridge Village

by Louisa Johnston

A ride on a time machine back to the days when the United States was a new country would be exciting. Visiting Old Sturbridge Village in Massachusetts is like taking a time-machine ride. Old Sturbridge Village is known as a living history museum. A living history museum is a museum that shows life as it used to be at a particular time and place in the past. Sturbridge Village is a good place to learn about country village life in early America.

Old Sturbridge Village was opened to visitors in 1946. Old Sturbridge Village is divided into sections: Center Village and Seasonal Exhibits; the Countryside and the Mill Neighborhood. The Center Village is made up of houses, meeting houses, the Printing Office, and a bank. The Countryside is made up of the District School, a Pottery Shop, a Blacksmith Shop, and farms. More than forty buildings of the kind that were built from 1790 to 1840 were brought in from places around New England. They were then moved onto the village land and put in working order.

At the village about four hundred people now live and work the same way that the people did who lived and worked in this part of America long ago. The people who live there today even dress as the people of early America dressed.

A visit to the Printing Shop would show workers setting books by hand just as printers of early America did. A press bangs slowly as pages of the book are printed. A rail is connected to the ceiling. The pages hang on the rail ready to dry. Some visitors say that the drying pages remind them of wash that is drying on a clothesline.

When children from other places visit Old Sturbridge Village, these children become part of the village. They attend the District School in the Countryside, which has only one room and one teacher. The children sit on wooden benches and share long wooden desks. They learn how to read, write, and count. Children practice their alphabet on small black slates. Girls wear bonnets and long dresses, and the boys wear shirts and trousers.

A worker is digging outside the Pottery Shop. When a visitor asks him what he is doing, the worker says that he is digging for clay. The clay is used to make plates, bowls, and cups. Each step in making them takes place in this shop.

The worker shows how he works with the clay and a wheel. The shape of a bowl appears as he works. When the bowl is completely formed, it will have to dry before it can be painted. After it is painted, the bowl is put into a special oven so it will harden. The oven is heated by wood that the worker has cut.

Bang! Bang! Bang! The sound of a worker's hammer as it hits iron can be heard everywhere in this part of the village. An excited group crowds around the Blacksmith Shop and watches the flashes of fire as the blacksmith pounds new farm tools into shape. The village farmers also bring all their broken farm tools to the Blacksmith Shop to be fixed.

A walk past the Blacksmith Shop leads to Freeman Farm. The village farmers can be seen plowing fields and growing crops which are used as food for the villagers. Farm animals are as important as the field crops. These farm animals provide food, transportation, power, and wool for making clothes.

When visitors leave Old Sturbridge Village, they feel they have come to know the people of early America much better. For at least one day, they have seen life as it was when our country began.

1. What makes Old Sturbridge Village seem real to visitors?

2. What do visitors learn about life in early New England?

3. How was Old Sturbridge Village built?

4. If you went to Old Sturbridge Village, what do you think you'd like best?

5. How does the author let you know that Old Sturbridge Village is a place to learn about early village life?

"Old Sturbridge Village" is an interesting story that tells or informs us about country village life in early America. Tell one important fact about each of the places in the village that is listed below.

1. Print Shop

2. Pottery Shop

3. Blacksmith Shop

Prewrite

Suppose you could take a ride in a time machine. To what year would you like to travel? Would you like to travel back in time, or would you like to travel ahead in time? Why? What things would be different from your life today?

Compose

Pretend you have a time machine. Choose a time and a place to which you would like to travel. Write a paragraph describing what life would be like. Tell how things are different in that time and place from the way they are where you live today.

Revise

Read your paragraph to make sure you have included all the information asked for in the activity. If changes are needed, make them.

Maps

Mr. Brown's third-grade class took a trip to Old Sturbridge Village. When they got to the village, Mr. Brown stopped at the Visitor Center to pick up a map to help the group find its way around the village. On the next page is the map they used.

Look at the map on page 249. It shows all of Old Sturbridge Village and has labels for the four sections. Notice that there is a small map placed in the corner of the large map. This small map is called an **inset map.** An inset map takes one portion of a map and enlarges that part to show more details. On this map of Old Sturbridge Village, the inset is showing, in detail, the section called Center Village. It shows and labels the houses and buildings found there. —Use the map of Old Sturbridge Village and the inset map of Center Village to answer the questions.

1. What building is between Thompson Bank and Fenno House?
2. What building is next to Gebhardt's Barn?
3. What building is between Salem Towne House and Fitch House?

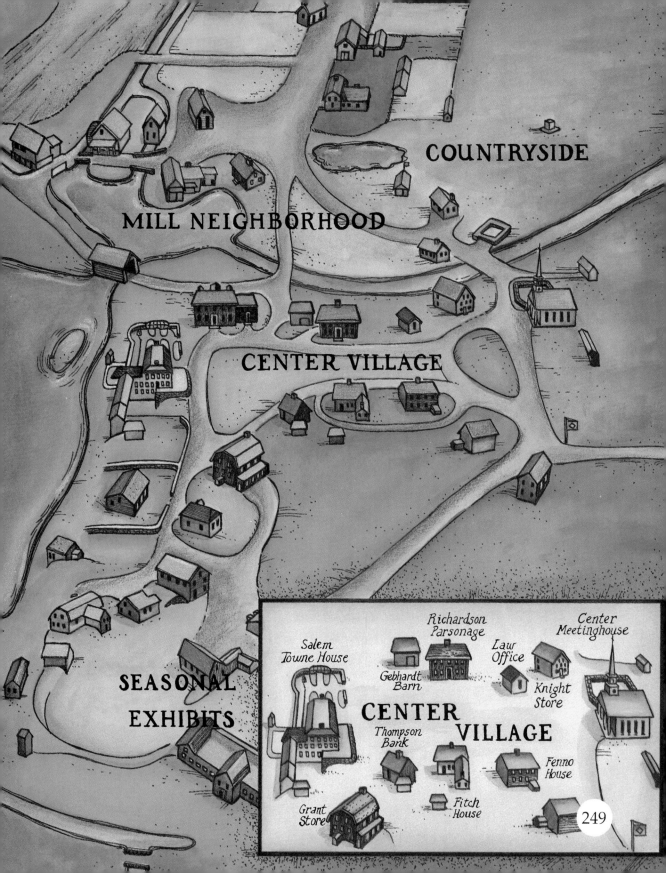

COUNTRYSIDE

MILL NEIGHBORHOOD

CENTER VILLAGE

SEASONAL EXHIBITS

Salem Towne House

Richardson Parsonage

Gebhardt Barn

Law Office

Center Meetinghouse

Knight Store

CENTER VILLAGE

Thompson Bank

Fenno House

Grant Store

Fitch House

249

Tall tales about John Henry have been told for many years. Why is John Henry remembered?

John Henry

by Anne Maley

In the 1870s, a man named John Henry came from Tennessee to work as a steel driver for the Chesapeake and Ohio Railroad in West Virginia. John Henry helped to build the Big Bend Tunnel through the West Virginia mountains. He died building that tunnel, after proving that a machine could not beat him at driving steel.

Ever since then, people have made up songs and stories, or tall tales, about John Henry, the steel-driving man. Through these songs and tales, people remember John Henry as a strong, brave man who had the spirit to say "I can do it" and who always did his best. This is one way that the story of John Henry is told.

Soon after John Henry was born, he reached out for his daddy's hammer hanging on the wall.

John Henry's father looked proudly at his son. "That boy is going to be a steel-driving man," he said. "I know it as surely as I know that rivers run to the sea."

John Henry was a few weeks old when he picked up his daddy's five-pound hammer and swung it in the air. Whoosh! Whoosh! Whoosh!

John Henry was only two months old when he began using the hammer to hit rocks in the yard. Bang! Bang! Bang! Then he told his mama, "I was born with a hammer in my hand. I was born to be a steel-driving man."

As a young man, John Henry was eight feet tall and had arms as big as tree trunks. He helped his mama around the house and his daddy on the farm. He could work harder and play harder than anyone around. It was not long before he began to think about going out into the world on his own.

251

Often John Henry would lie in bed at night and listen to the long, lonely sounds of the trains going by. He dreamed about working on a railroad somewhere, using a big hammer to drive steel.

One night John Henry told his mama and daddy about a dream he had. "I was working on the railroad," John Henry said. "I was swinging my mighty hammer and driving steel right into the ground. When I swung it in the air, a rainbow circled around my shoulder. When my hammer hit the spike, sparks flew into the sky."

The next morning, John Henry said good-bye to his mama and daddy. Then he left to find his own way in the world. He knew he could do any work and do it well. He just had to find the right job for him.

John Henry found his first work on farms and in cotton fields. He became the best cotton picker in the South. He could pick three bales of cotton a day, more than any other worker. He wanted work that paid better, so he found a job on a riverboat that traveled the river carrying goods from place to place. Yet all the while he was thinking about that hammer and waiting for his time to come.

While working on the riverboat, John Henry heard that the Chesapeake and Ohio Railroad needed workers. They wanted strong men who could help build the Big Bend Tunnel through the mountains in West Virginia. John Henry left his job on the riverboat and headed for West Virginia.

On the way there he met a girl named Polly Ann. She was the prettiest girl he had ever seen. Soon he and Polly Ann were married, and they set off to West Virginia. As they were walking through the mountains, John Henry heard a sweet sound. "Listen, Polly Ann," he said. "It's the sound of hammers striking steel!" So they followed the sounds until there it was—the C & O Railroad! The railroad tracks ran right up to the foot of a huge, rocky mountain and then stopped.

John Henry watched the men work. He watched a man called a *shaker* hold a steel spike in place on the rock. He watched another man swing his ten-pound hammer in the air and whomp the steel into the stone. Again and again, the steel driver drove the steel deeper into the rock. When the hole was deep enough, another man put explosives in the hole to blow the rock away. Little by little, the tunnel would be blown out of the mountain.

John Henry walked over to the boss, Captain Tommy, and said, "I'm John Henry, a steel-driving man, and I'm looking for a job."

"You're big, but what do you know about driving steel?" asked Captain Tommy.

"I'm a natural man," answered John Henry. "Driving steel is just a natural thing for me to do."

"Then take this twenty-pound hammer," said Captain Tommy. "We'll see what a natural man can do. I'll even give you my best steel shaker, Little Will, to hold the spike."

As Little Will held the spike, John Henry swung the twenty-pound hammer high over his head. Then he brought the hammer down and it landed in the middle of the spike, sending the spike halfway into the rock. John Henry swung again, and this time the spike went all the way into the rock.

Neither Little Will nor Captain Tommy could believe their eyes. "I've never seen a man drive a spike so far in two blows," said Captain Tommy. "John Henry, you're hired!"

After that, Little Will and John Henry worked together every day. John Henry swung his mighty hammer, and Little Will held the spikes. John Henry sang as he worked, and Little Will sang along:

There ain't no hammer upon this mountain
Rings like mine, boys, rings like mine.
This old hammer rings like silver,
Shines like gold, boys, shines like gold.

After a while, John Henry began swinging two twenty-pound hammers, one in each hand. People came from miles around to watch him work and hear him sing.

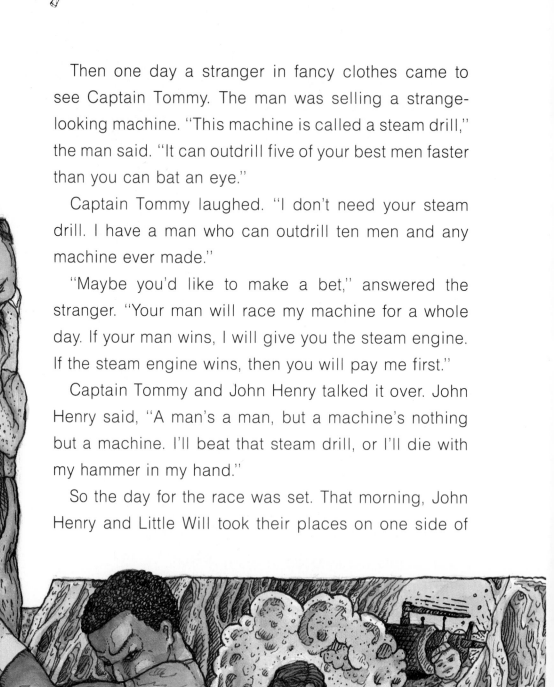

Then one day a stranger in fancy clothes came to see Captain Tommy. The man was selling a strange-looking machine. "This machine is called a steam drill," the man said. "It can outdrill five of your best men faster than you can bat an eye."

Captain Tommy laughed. "I don't need your steam drill. I have a man who can outdrill ten men and any machine ever made."

"Maybe you'd like to make a bet," answered the stranger. "Your man will race my machine for a whole day. If your man wins, I will give you the steam engine. If the steam engine wins, then you will pay me first."

Captain Tommy and John Henry talked it over. John Henry said, "A man's a man, but a machine's nothing but a machine. I'll beat that steam drill, or I'll die with my hammer in my hand."

So the day for the race was set. That morning, John Henry and Little Will took their places on one side of the tunnel. The steam drill was on the other side. Polly Ann joined the crowd who had gathered around the tunnel to watch. When the judge blew his whistle, the race began. Soon the tunnel walls shook with the chug and clatter of the steam drill and the whoosh and clang of John Henry's hammer striking steel.

The race went on and on in the hot, dark tunnel. The whole mountain rang with the chug and clatter and clang of man and machine driving steel. Only once did the machine break down and need to have a worn part replaced. Only once did John Henry stop to get water.

Just when it seemed that the noise and the drilling would never end, the judge blew the whistle. The race was over.

The judge examined the drilling holes and declared, "John Henry drilled the most holes and the deepest holes. He has beaten the machine!" The people clapped and cheered.

Polly Ann ran to John Henry and found him lying on the ground with a hammer in his hand. The doctor who examined him said, "His heart just stopped. John Henry, the natural steel-driving man, died with a hammer in his hand."

1. Why do people remember John Henry?

2. What happened when John Henry raced the steam drill?

3. Who do you think really won the contest? Why?

4. What helps you to know what John Henry meant when he said "I'm a natural man"?

5. Find two examples of colorful language that the author uses in the story.

We have learned that the story "John Henry" is a tall tale. A *tall tale* is a story that is not true. Characters in tall tales are made to seem bigger or faster or stronger than they could be in the real world. For example, we know that John Henry did not really pick up a five-pound hammer when he was a few weeks old.

On page 251, find at least two things about John Henry that make this story a tall tale.

Prewrite

Think about why "John Henry" is a tall tale. Then think about writing a tall tale of your own. Who would your character be? What two things would this character be able to do that could not be done in the real world?

Compose

Choose one of the activities below.

1. Write another tall tale about John Henry. In your story, tell some other jobs that John Henry could do that a character in the real world could not do.

2. Write a tall tale about a make-believe person. Make sure you include enough ideas that make your story a tall tale.

Revise

Check your work to make sure you have written a tall tale. Your story should have a beginning, a middle, and an ending. It should make sense to the person reading it even though it is a tall tale. If changes are needed, make them.

It Couldn't Be Done

by *Edgar A. Guest*

Somebody said that it couldn't be done,
    But he with a chuckle replied
That "maybe it couldn't," but he would be one
    Who wouldn't say so till he'd tried.
So he buckled right in with the trace of a grin
    On his face. If he worried he hid it.
He started to sing as he tackled the thing
    That couldn't be done, and he did it.

Cause and Effect

In some stories, authors tell you how one thing causes another thing to happen. The **cause** tells why something happens. The **effect,** or result, is what happens.

Read the following sentences. Then read the answers to the questions below.

Louis practiced throwing a baseball every day. He became a very good pitcher.

What happened because Louis practiced every day? He became a very good pitcher. *He became a very good pitcher* is the effect. Why did this happen? Louis practiced throwing a baseball every day. *Practicing throwing a baseball every day* is the cause of Louis's becoming a good pitcher.

In the sentences about Louis, there was one cause that led to one effect. Often there may be several causes that lead to one effect.

Read the story that follows. Look for the three causes that lead to one effect.

Katie was going to meet her friend, Jenny, for lunch at twelve o'clock.

As Katie was leaving her house, the phone rang. She talked for ten minutes. Then, she rushed to the car and saw that the tire was flat. It took her twenty minutes to change the tire. When Katie got to the restaurant, there were no parking places nearby. So she parked her car three blocks away and walked to the restaurant. When she looked at her watch, she saw that it was one o'clock. Katie was one hour late.

What happened in this story? Katie was one hour late for lunch. This is the *effect*. What are the three reasons that caused Katie to be late? She talked on the phone, she had a flat tire, and she could not find a close parking place.

Remember that authors often use cause and effect to connect ideas. Remember also that several causes can lead to one effect. Looking for these cause-effect relationships will help you understand what you have read.

Going to a new school causes special problems for Mike. Who helps Mike solve some of these problems? How?

A Contest

by Sherry Neuwirth Payne

Mike is ten. He's in fifth grade. He used to go to a special school where all his friends had crutches or wheelchairs like his. He and his friends did a lot of fun things in their wheelchairs. Sometimes they had races in their wheelchairs. Mike likes races and games.

What Mike doesn't like is people who stare at
him. Mike's legs don't work. He wears braces on his
legs. Since Mike can't use his legs, he will always
need a wheelchair.

Now Mike is at a new school. Here Mike needs
help with some things. The cartons of milk in the
cafeteria are too far away for Mike to reach without
spilling the tray in his lap. Mike also needs help
with all the doors. At first he was afraid to ask anyone for help. Everyone seemed to stare at him.

On the first day of school a boy named Randy
grabbed Mike's orange baseball hat and ran away
with it. Mike hated his new school.

When Mike told his dad about it, his dad said,
"It's not easy, is it, Mike? You have to live with all
kinds of people. A good place to start learning
about them is in school." Mike said he'd still go,
but he wouldn't like it.

Mike's teacher, Mrs. Kocher, must have noticed
his sad face, because one day she asked Mike to
stay after school.

"Mike," she said, "you don't like this school very
much, do you?"

"I sure don't, Mrs. Kocher," Mike said. "I'm the
only kid in a wheelchair. I feel so different."

"I'll bet you do," Mrs. Kocher said. "What we need to do is show the other kids the ways you're not so different. I have an idea. What can you do especially well?"

"Well, I'm really good at checkers," said Mike. "I play with my father almost every day, and I'm good at arm wrestling."

"Arm wrestling?" said Mrs. Kocher. "That might be just the thing. We could have a contest. There are some pretty strong kids in this class, especially Randy."

"I'm sure I could win if you'd just give me a chance," Mike said.

"Why don't you try me first," said Mrs. Kocher. "See if you can beat me."

It didn't take long for Mike to push Mrs. Kocher's arm to the table. Mrs. Kocher looked a little surprised. Then she winked at Mike. "Arm wrestling it is then," she said with a smile.

The next day when all the children were at their desks, Mrs. Kocher asked, "Who would like to have an arm-wrestling contest today?" Every hand in the room shot up.

"Good. Susan and Mary, would you like to start?" Susan and Mary sat at the table facing each other.

They put their elbows on the table and locked hands. "One, two, three, go!" Mrs. Kocher said.

Each person took a turn with the winner. Randy won his first match easily. He won every match after that, too. Finally everyone had taken a turn and Randy was still at the table.

"Now it's your turn, Mike. Would you like to try?" asked Mrs. Kocher.

"Arm wrestle him?" Randy said. "But I'll probably hurt him."

"Just try me," Mike said. He was nervous, but he smiled at Randy.

At first Randy looked as if he was afraid to touch Mike. Then they locked hands and put their elbows on the table. "One, two, three, go!" Mrs. Kocher said.

Then Mike pushed Randy's arm down to the table in a second. Randy looked surprised. "I just didn't want to hurt you," Randy said. "Let's do that again."

The second time was a little harder, but Mike finally pushed Randy's arm over again. Mike had a warm feeling inside. He felt scared, too. What if Randy was mad at him for winning?

"My arms are really strong from pushing my wheelchair around," Mike told Randy.

"No kidding," said Randy.

"It looks like the arm-wrestling champion of this class is Mike Stevens," Mrs. Kocher announced. "Tomorrow we'll have a checkers contest."

At the end of the day Randy walked over to Mike and said, "I suppose you're good at checkers, too?"

"I'm okay," said Mike. "At my old school we played checkers every day."

"Well, you may have won the arm-wrestling contest, but I play checkers with my sister. I always win." Randy went to meet his friends.

The next day in the cafeteria Susan sat down beside Mike. "Want a push back to the room?" she asked.

"Thanks, but I can push myself," answered Mike. "I wouldn't mind some company, though."

"Are you good enough to win at checkers, too?" Susan asked.

"I'm sure going to try," said Mike.

The checkers contest started right after lunch. Mike thought about every move he made. Finally it was just Mike and Randy. Then it was over, and Mrs. Kocher announced the winner. "Mike Stevens is our checkers champion. You gave him a good battle though, Randy." She smiled at both of them. Randy was smiling, too.

"What else can you do?" Randy asked Mike.

1. Why didn't Mike like his new school?
2. How did Mrs. Kocher help Mike?
3. What happened that changed how Mike felt?
4. What kind of person do you think Mike is?
5. When did you know that Mike would win the arm-wrestling match?

Apply the Skills

When we read a story, we find out that certain things cause other things to happen. In "A Contest," there are many causes and effects. Read each cause below. Tell what the effect of each cause is. Use the story as a guide. Then find another cause and effect in the story.

1. Because Mike can't use his legs, he ▬▬▬.
2. Because Mrs. Kocher noticed Mike's sad face, she ▬▬▬.
3. Mike was good at checkers because ▬▬▬.
4. Mike was good at arm wrestling because ▬▬▬.

Prewrite

In "A Contest," a boy named Mike had to use a wheelchair because his legs didn't work. The *effect* is what happened: *Mike had to use a wheelchair.* The *cause* is why it happened: *Mike's legs didn't work.* Do you think Mike and Randy will become friends?

Compose

Choose one of the activities below.

1. Read the following effect: *Mike did not like his new school.* Write a paragraph that describes the cause for Mike's dislike of school. Tell at least three reasons why Mike did not like his new school.

2. At the end of the story, Randy asked Mike, "What else can you do?" Do you think Mike and Randy will become friends? Write a paragraph that tells why.

Revise

Read your paragraph carefully. Be sure you have followed the directions. If changes are needed, make them.

Outlines

Before the author of "Old Sturbridge Village" could write the article, she had to organize the information. She knew that the **topic** of the article would be Sturbridge Village. She decided that she would write about the history of the village, Center Village, and the Countryside. These would be her **main topics.** If the author had made an outline before writing the article, this is what it would have looked like:

Old Sturbridge Village
I.   History
II. Center Village
III. Countryside

"Old Sturbridge Village" is the title, or topic, of the outline. The main topics are "History," "Center Village," and "Countryside."

The author decided to add information to each main topic. In the following outline, the additional facts are called the **subtopics.** Notice that there is a capital letter before each subtopic. Notice also that each capital letter is directly under the first letter of the first word of each main topic.

Old Sturbridge Village	Topic
I. History	I. Main topic
A. Opened in 1946	A. Subtopic
B. Is a living history museum	B. Subtopic
II. Center Village	II. Main topic
A. Printing Shop	A. Subtopic
B. Other stores	B. Subtopic
III. Countryside	III. Main topic
A. District School	A. Subtopic
B. Pottery Shop	B. Subtopic
C. Blacksmith Shop	C. Subtopic
D. Farms	D. Subtopic

This is the outline the author might have used when the article was written. Outlines can be useful in several ways. They can help you organize information before you write. They can also help you organize information that you've read so you can remember it.

Textbook Application: Outlining in Social Studies

Read this article from a textbook. Use the side-notes to find the topic, main topics, and subtopics.

This title tells you the topic of the article.

This heading tells you the first main topic.

This paragraph contains sub-topics. The two subtopics are *buses* and *trains*.

This heading is the second main topic.

The first paragraph tells you about one sub-topic. What is that subtopic?

The second paragraph contains the second sub-topic. What is it?

COMMUNITY SERVICES

Transportation Services

Do you take a city bus to school? If so, you are using public transportation. Buses and trains are two kinds of public transportation. They are another kind of service many communities provide to people. People pay money when they ride public transportation.

Health Services

Many communities have hospitals to care for people who are very hurt or sick. Most hospitals have emergency rooms. People can get help right away at a hospital emergency room.

Community clinics are also places that treat people who are hurt or ill. At many clinics there are doctors and dentists who can take care of the whole family.

Public Schools

One community service you know about is the public school system. Most communities have a board of education. Its members are elected by the people of the community.

In many communities, it is up to the board of education to help choose teachers. The board decides how the schools should be run. The board does an important job. A good education gives people a good start in life.

—*Communities,* Harcourt Brace Jovanovich

What is this heading?

What is the sub-topic in this paragraph?

Teachers is the subtopic in this paragraph.

An outline of the article would look like this:

Community Services

I. Transportation
   A. Buses
   B. Trains
II. Health Services
   A. Hospitals
   B. Clinics
III. Public Schools
   A. Board of Education
   B. Teachers

The main topic in an outline gives the most important point. The subtopics give details.

Who is Eleanor Roosevelt? Why is she still remembered?

Eleanor Roosevelt

by Jane Goodsell

Eleanor Roosevelt was a niece of President Theodore Roosevelt. Both her parents had died when she was very young so, while Eleanor was growing up, she lived with her grandmother. Eleanor's grandmother did not think children needed playmates. Eleanor spent most of her day studying French, music, and sewing. She had very few friends.

As Eleanor grew older, she began to go to parties and dances. Since Eleanor was shy, she often sat by herself and wished she were at home reading a book. Eleanor did not make friends easily. At one party she met a distant cousin named Franklin Roosevelt. They soon became good friends. In 1905, when Eleanor was twenty-one years old, she and Franklin were married.

While Eleanor was raising a family, Franklin was busy in politics. He was elected to the New York State Senate, he was the Assistant Secretary of the Navy, and he ran for vice-president of the United States in 1920.

One summer day in 1921, while on vacation at Campobello Island, Franklin felt sick. Three days later the doctor said Franklin had polio. As a result of this illness, Franklin's leg muscles became very weak, and it was impossible for him to walk.

The doctors said that Franklin would have to wear leg braces for the rest of his life and use a wheelchair. Franklin made up his mind that he would not spend his life in a wheelchair. He exercised to make his arms stronger so he could use crutches.

As Franklin grew stronger, Eleanor knew that she must make sure that he would go back to politics. Fighting her shyness, Eleanor began to make speeches so that people would not forget the Roosevelt name.

A few years later, he was elected governor of the State of New York. Eleanor continued to help Franklin. Where he could not go on his crutches, she went in his place. She would tell Franklin what she had seen and heard.

In 1932, Franklin was elected President of the United States. Eleanor turned out to be a very good First Lady. Wherever there were people in the country who needed help, Eleanor Roosevelt went to see what could be done for them.

During the Second World War, American soldiers
were sent to many parts of the world. Eleanor Roosevelt traveled thousands of miles to visit them. She
went to cheer up the soldiers who were far from
home and lonely.

In 1945, a few months after he began his fourth
term as President, Franklin died. His death shocked
the world. Eleanor was no longer the First Lady but
she knew she must stay busy. She worked for justice
and freedom for people everywhere. She continued
to travel far and wide. Wherever she went, she met
old friends and made new ones. She was a famous
woman, and people everywhere felt that she was
their friend.

Eleanor was seventy-eight years old when she died
in 1962. Millions of people all over the world cried at
the news of her death. The little girl who had few
friends had grown up to be known and loved by
people all over the world.

1. Why do people still remember Eleanor Roosevelt?

2. Why were so many people sad when Eleanor Roosevelt died?

3. How did Eleanor Roosevelt's life change after her husband became sick with polio?

4. Why do you think Eleanor Roosevelt was loved by people all over the world?

5. How did the author show that Eleanor Roosevelt changed?

Think about the biography of Eleanor Roosevelt. What was the most interesting fact you learned about Eleanor Roosevelt? Complete each sentence below with another fact you learned.

1. When she was a little girl, ▬▬▬.

2. When her husband was getting better, ▬▬▬.

3. When she was the First Lady, ▬▬▬.

Prewrite

The selection you have just read is a biography because it tells about a person's life. Think about an interesting or famous person you know. What makes this person interesting?

Compose

Choose one of the following activities.

1. Write a paragraph that tells facts about an interesting or famous person you know. Your paragraph should tell at least four facts about the person's life and should tell why this person is interesting or famous.

2. Write a paragraph that tells how Eleanor Roosevelt came to be known and loved by people all over the world. Your paragraph should describe at least three reasons why people knew and loved Eleanor Roosevelt.

Revise

Check your work. Did you follow the directions given? If changes are needed, make them.

The Ordinary Kid
by George E. Coon

Ryan is an ordinary kid like you
Who dreams of extraordinary things to do.

That's why he'll wrestle a lion one day,
And swim the Pacific; all the way.

Being an ordinary kid, of course,
He'll run a race and beat a horse.

He'll win the national spelling bee
By spelling Massachusetts and Tennessee.

He'll climb a mountain to the top.
Others will try, but have to stop.

He'll play a concert at Carnegie Hall;
They'll pack people in from wall to wall.

He'll shoot the basket to win the game,
And everyone will shout his name.

There's nothing that Ryan won't be able to do.
He's an ordinary kid, just like you.

283

What kind of person is Miss Graham?
What does she do that causes Michael to
want to stay with her?

The Boy Who Wanted a Family

by Shirley Gordon

Michael had lived in many foster homes. He did not know his natural parents. Miss Finch was the social worker who helped Michael when he moved from one foster home to another.

One day Miss Finch took Michael to see Miss Graham. Miss Graham liked Michael and wanted to adopt him. Michael went to live with Miss Graham and began to call her Mom.

"What's the matter?" his mom asked.

"I don't want to do my homework," Michael said. Then he told her that he was supposed to write a story about his family.

"You have a grandpa who lives in Florida," said his mom.

"I do?" Michael was surprised.

"My father is your grandpa," his mom explained. "Maybe someday we can take a trip and meet him."

"Do I have a grandma, too?" asked Michael.

His mom shook her head. "No, your grandma died before you came here. It's too bad, honey—she would have loved you very much."

Michael frowned. "I don't have enough to write."

"Don't worry—eat your spaghetti," said his mom. "Then, first thing after dinner, you can help me write a letter to Kim Soo[1] and Kim Joong[2]."

"Who?" asked Michael.

"They're my two foster children in Korea," said his mom. "That means they're your foster brothers."

"Hooray!" cheered Michael. "I don't have to make up brothers."

She explained, "Kim Soo is ten years old, and Kim Joong is thirteen. They both like to play baseball. You can write and tell them you like to play football."

"I like baseball, too," said Michael.

As soon as they finished dinner, they went into Michael's room. His mom showed him Korea on his map of the world. "I bet nobody else in school has two brothers who live across the ocean," thought Michael.

"After we finish writing the letter, I'm going to do my homework," he said.

---

[1] Kim Soo [kim sōō]
[2] Kim Joong [kim jŏŏng]

The next morning before he went to school, Michael gave his cat, Motorboat, a fresh bowl of milk. He put a drop of water and a piece of lemon leaf into the ant farm his mom had bought for him. Just then, he thought of something more to write on his paper.

As soon as he got to school, he gave his paper to the teacher. The teacher read it. Then she read it again — out loud to the whole class.

My Family

I have a new mother who is very nice. I have a black cat who makes a noise like a motorboat, so that is what I call her. My grandma is not alive and my grandpa is in Florida. I have two big brothers in Korea who play baseball. I also have six ants.

"My goodness, Michael," said the teacher. "You have an interesting family."

"Thanks," said Michael.

"There's only one thing," said the teacher. "The correct way to spell 'aunt' is *a-u-n-t*."

Michael smiled. "That's not the way to spell the ants in my family." He spoke about his ant farm.

"You do have a very interesting family, Michael," said the teacher.

After school Albert and Benny walked part way home with Michael.

"You wrote the best paper in the whole class," said Albert.

"You're lucky," said Benny. "We only have ordinary aunts in my family."

Michael felt proud. He wished that he had a family like everybody else, but, at the same time, he liked being different. He waved good-bye to Albert and Benny at the corner and turned down his street.

The first thing he saw was Miss Finch's car parked in front of his house. Michael's stomach began to ache. "She's going to take me away to another foster home," Michael thought. He wished he could hide someplace. It was getting cold out, and pretty soon it would get dark. Miss Finch would probably hang around forever, waiting to take him away.

Maybe he could sneak inside the house and hide in his room. Michael went up the front walk quietly and tiptoed to the front door to listen. He couldn't hear anything. Slowly, he turned the knob and opened the door, hoping it wouldn't squeak.

His mom and Miss Finch were talking in the kitchen. If only he could tiptoe into his room without being seen. As soon as he took the first step—*cre-eak*! The floor squeaked under his sneakers.

"Michael?" called his mom.

It was no use. Now his mom would come looking for him. He gave up and went into the kitchen.

Miss Finch smiled at him. "Hello, Michael."

"H'lo."

"How are you getting along?"

"Fine!" he answered in a loud voice.

Michael began to feel uncomfortable. "Even if she tries to take me away," Michael thought, "I won't go. She couldn't pick me up and carry me. I'm too big."

Motorboat came into the kitchen. "That's my cat," said Michael. "Her name is Motorboat."

"Hello, Motorboat," said Miss Finch.

"She hasn't said anything about taking me away," thought Michael. "Maybe she came to tell me I'm adopted now."

"I have a lot of new friends," he said, thinking about Albert and Benny at school, and Tony and Peter down the street.

Miss Finch smiled. "It sounds as though you're getting along fine, all right."

"We're both getting along fine," Michael's mom said.

"That's good to hear," said Miss Finch.

"Am I adopted now?" asked Michael anxiously. Miss Finch shook her head. "No, Michael—not yet. You have to wait a whole year."

"A whole year?" asked Michael. By then, his mom might change her mind and not want to keep him anymore. He remembered the family he'd liked who had almost adopted him. Even nice people change their minds if they want to.

His mom gave him a hug. "Don't worry," she said. "The year will go very fast."

Discuss

the

Selection

1. Why did Michael want to stay with Miss Graham?

2. Why didn't Michael want to wait a year to be adopted?

3. Why was Michael afraid to go home when he saw Miss Finch's car?

4. How did you feel when Miss Graham said, "The year will go very fast"?

5. When did you know that Michael would be able to do his homework?

Apply

the

Skills

Think about "The Boy Who Wanted a Family." Then answer each question below.

1. What caused Michael to name his cat Motorboat?

2. What caused Michael's friends to think Michael had an interesting family?

3. What was the effect of Michael's wanting to be adopted right away?

Prewrite

The children in Michael's class thought his family was interesting. What makes Michael's family interesting? Think about why Michael would want to be adopted by Miss Graham.

Compose

Choose one of the activities below.

1. Imagine that you are in Michael's class at school. Write a story about a family. It may be a real or make-believe family. Tell about each member of the family and what makes each one special. If you wish, you may draw a picture of the family you have described.

2. Pretend that you are Michael. Write a letter to Miss Finch telling her why you want to be adopted by Miss Graham. Use the correct form for writing a letter.

Revise

Read your work carefully. Does it really say what you want it to say? Make any changes that are needed.

What are all the clues that Cam Jansen used to solve this case? What mystery does Cam solve?

The Mystery of the Television Dog

by David A. Adler

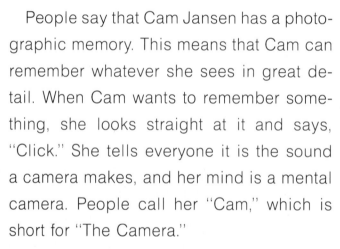

People say that Cam Jansen has a photographic memory. This means that Cam can remember whatever she sees in great detail. When Cam wants to remember something, she looks straight at it and says, "Click." She tells everyone it is the sound a camera makes, and her mind is a mental camera. People call her "Cam," which is short for "The Camera."

In this story, Cam Jansen, her friend Eric, and Eric's twin sisters, Donna and Diane, are in front of Lee's Bookstore, waiting to meet Poochie, the famous television dog.

Poochie, a white dog with black spots across his back, walked into the bookstore. His trainer followed him. Cam wanted to remember Poochie. She looked straight at the dog and said, "Click."

Cam, Eric, and the twins looked through the bookstore window. They saw Poochie jump onto a table. He sat down between the pile of books and the Poochie photograph. Mr. Lee, the bookstore owner, called out, "Say hello to Poochie. You can shake his paw. If you buy *The Poochie Story,* Poochie will autograph it for you."

Poochie's trainer opened an ink pad and put it on the table next to the book. Poochie pressed one of his paws onto the ink pad, and then he pressed it onto the front page of the book.

The line was moving slowly. A small boy walked out of the bookstore with his mother. The boy said, "Poochie signed my book!" The boy's mother held up her hand for everyone to see. There was ink on it. She said, "Poochie shook my hand."

When Cam, Eric, Donna and Diane were inside the bookstore, they saw a red-haired man holding a white dog with black spots that looked just like Poochie. The man reached into his pocket, and, as he did, a box of dog biscuits fell onto the table. The man's dog jumped after the biscuits, and Poochie jumped, too. The dogs started barking and then chased each other around the table. Then the red-haired man grabbed a dog.

"Bad, Cloudy, bad," he said as he left the bookstore with his dog.

"Now sit, Poochie," the trainer said, but the dog didn't sit. "Sit!" the trainer said again. The dog barked and wagged his tail, but he didn't sit.

"I'm next, I'm next," Donna told Mr. Lee. Donna smiled at the dog. Diane and Cam shook Poochie's paw, and Eric bought a copy of *The Poochie Story*.

As they left the store, Donna said, "I'm hungry."

"Before you eat, you have to wash your hands," Eric told her. "You just shook Poochie's paw."

Donna held out her hands. "My hands are clean."

"Let me see," Cam said as she looked at Donna's hands and then at her own hands.

"That's strange," Cam said. Cam ran back to the bookstore, and Eric, Donna, and Diane followed her. Cam looked through the bookstore window, closed her eyes, and said, "Click."

"What's she doing?" Diane whispered to Eric.

"She's trying to remember something."

Cam opened her eyes and looked through the window again. "I was right. The dog in there is not Poochie. The picture I have of Poochie in my mind and the dog in the bookstore are not the same."

"That dog looks like Poochie to me," Eric said.

"The spots on that dog are not in the exact same places as the spots on Poochie," Cam said.

Donna ran into the bookstore. "That's not Poochie! That's not Poochie!" she yelled.

"Of course it is. Just watch." The trainer said, "Poochie, raise your right paw." The dog just looked at the trainer. "Raise your right paw!" the trainer said again. The dog did nothing.

Cam pointed to the photograph of Poochie and said, "Look at this and look at the dog. You'll see that they're not the same."

"It was that red-haired man," Eric said. "He must have taken Poochie. This must be Cloudy."

"Well, I'm calling the police," Mr. Lee said. As Mr. Lee walked toward the telephone, Cloudy jumped off the table and ran out of the bookstore.

"Get him!" Mr. Lee told Cam, Eric, and the twins.

The children all ran after Cloudy. They followed him past a shopping mall and through a backyard to the front porch of a house.

"I knew he'd lead us to his house," Cam said. "I think we'll find Poochie and the red-haired man in there."

"Here, Cloudy," Cam called. Cloudy turned and ran to Cam. Just as Cloudy reached Cam, the front door of the house opened. The children were near a large bush. They hid behind it.

"Who's there?" a man called out.

Cam looked straight at the man and said, "Click." He

was bald, tall, heavy, and wore eyeglasses. The man waited a minute and then went back into the house.

"I don't think Poochie is here," Eric whispered. "The man we saw in the bookstore, the one who took Poochie, had red hair. The man who just came to the door was bald."

Cam closed her eyes and said, "Click." She thought for a short while. Then she said, "I'm looking at the picture I have in my memory of the man we saw in the bookstore. He looks like the man we just saw. Only the hair is different."

Just then the front door opened. The bald man came out carrying a large bag. Cam looked through the bush and watched as he turned it over. Boxes, papers, and something red fell into the trash can.

"Did you see that?" Cam whispered. "You watch Cloudy. I'm going to get something." Cam walked across the front lawn to the trash can. She reached in and took out something red.

When Cam got back she said, "The man in the bookstore had red hair and here it is. The man inside the house wore this wig so people wouldn't know who he was. He's the one who took Poochie."

"What are we going to do?" Diane asked.

Cam thought, and then she said, "We will have to try to switch the dogs. If Donna taps on one window, the man will run over to see who's there. Then Diane can tap on another window, and the man will run to that window. If you two take turns tapping on windows, the man will be busy running from one to the other. That's when I'll switch the dogs through that open window."

Donna walked up to one of the windows at the side of the house, and Diane went to another window near the front door. *Tap. Tap.* It was Donna tapping at the window. The man went to see who it was.

Tap. Tap. It was Diane tapping at the other window. Cam heard the man run to the other window. "This is my chance," thought Cam. She let Cloudy jump through the open window. Then she called, "Here, Poochie."

Cam saw Poochie jump onto a desk, grab a green envelope in his mouth, and then jump off.

"Stay away from my house!" yelled the man. Just then Poochie jumped onto the windowsill. Then he jumped into Cam's arms. Cam took the envelope out of his mouth and put it into her pocket. They all headed back to Lee's Bookstore.

"We have Poochie," Donna told Mr. Lee as they walked into the bookstore.

Two police officers were standing there with Mr. Lee and Poochie's trainer. One of them asked, "Where's the man who took him?" Cam told them where the man lived and they went to pick him up. When they came back, the bald man was with them.

"I thought he was Cloudy," the man said.

Poochie walked across the table to Cam. With his mouth, Poochie took the green envelope out of Cam's pocket and took it to one of the police officers. The police officers opened the envelope.

"It's a note. It says that you will give Poochie back only after some money is paid. You took Poochie. You're coming with us."

"These children should get a reward," Mr. Lee said.

"Yes, they should," the trainer said. He reached into his pocket and took out a small card. Poochie pressed his paw onto the ink pad and then onto the card. "This is a pass for all of you to come to our studio and watch a Poochie television program being taped."

Then Eric asked, "Could the real Poochie autograph our book?" Poochie pressed his paw onto the ink pad and then onto the book. At the door the children waved to Poochie.

"Woof . . . woof," Poochie barked, and wagged his tail.

1. What mystery did Cam solve?

2. How did Cam's photographic memory help solve this mystery?

3. What was the reward for solving the mystery?

4. Do you think it was a good reward?

5. When did you know that the bald man was not telling the truth?

When we read a story, we draw conclusions using the details in the story. Cam and her friends used the details in this story to solve the mystery. They drew a conclusion based on clues in the story.

1. Find two clues on page 297.

2. Find another clue on page 299.

Prewrite

In "The Mystery of the Television Dog," Cam's photographic memory and the details in the story helped the children solve the mystery. Imagine that you are looking for a missing lunch. Think about the kinds of clues you might find while trying to solve the mystery.

Compose

Choose one of the activities below.

1. Pretend that you have been asked to tell about the missing lunch. Write a list of clues that tell how you would solve the mystery.

2. Write a paragraph describing a lunch that is missing. Include at least four sentences that tell about the lunch so that another person might be able to help you find it.

Revise

Check your work carefully. Does your paragraph include enough information to make your description clear to the person reading it? If not, add more details to your description.

How does a horseback ride teach Ellen a lesson?
What is the lesson that she learns?

Ellen Rides Again

by Beverly Cleary

Ellen Tebbits and Austine Allen were best friends. They liked doing many things together.

Austine read many books about horses and wanted to ride one. Ellen didn't know much about horses but had ridden several times. As the story begins, the girls are at the library talking about horses.

At the library Austine had been lucky enough to find two horse books. "I wish I could ride a horse sometime," she said.

"Haven't you ever ridden a horse?" asked Ellen.

"No. Have you?" Austine sounded impressed.

"Oh, yes," said Ellen casually. "Several times."

It was true. She had ridden several times. If she had ridden twice, she would have said a couple of times. Three was several times, so she had told the truth.

"Where? What was it like? Tell me about it," begged Austine.

"Oh, different places." That was also true. She had ridden at the beach. Her father had rented a horse for an hour and had let Ellen ride behind him with her arms around his waist. The horse's back had been slippery, and she had bounced harder than was comfortable, but she had been able to hang on.

She had ridden at Uncle Fred's farm. Uncle Fred had lifted her up onto the back of his old plow horse, Lady, and led her twice around the barnyard. Lady didn't bounce her at all.

Then there was that other time when her father had paid a dime so she could ride a pony around in a circle inside a fence. It hadn't been very exciting. The pony seemed tired, but Ellen had pretended it was galloping madly. Yes, it all added up to several times.

"Why haven't you told me you could ride?" Austine demanded. "What kind of saddle do you use?" Austine knew all about different kinds of saddles because she read so many horse books.

"Oh, any kind," said Ellen, who did not know one saddle from another. "Once I rode bareback." That was true, because Lady had no saddle. Ellen was beginning to feel a little uncomfortable. She had not meant to mislead Austine. She really did not know how it all started.

The next day at school Austine did not forget what Ellen had said about being able to ride a horse. She told Linda and Amelia about it. They told Barbara and George. Barbara and George told other boys and girls. Each time the story was told, it grew.

After school, when the girls came to Austine's house, they found Mrs. Allen on her knees beside a box of plants. "Hello there," she said. "Since tomorrow is Memorial Day and there isn't any school, how would you like to go on a picnic? Ellen, I have already asked your mother and she says you may go."

"Thank you. I'd love to go." Maybe a picnic would make Austine forget about horses. Ellen was worried that Austine might say something about horseback riding to Ellen's mother, and her mother would know how Ellen had exaggerated.

The next morning at ten o'clock Ellen ran down Tillamook Street and around the corner to Austine's house. Mr. Allen was backing out the car. Mrs. Allen sat in the front seat. Ellen was glad she and Austine could each sit by a window in the back. That made it easier to look for horses and to play word games.

They had only driven a few miles when Austine saw the horses. "Look, Daddy! Horses for rent! Please stop," she begged.

Mr. Allen drew over to the side of the road near some horses in a corral. Austine jumped out of the car and ran to the horses, while the others followed.

"Daddy, please let us go horseback riding!" Ellen wished Austine would keep still.

"All right, girls. Which horses do you want to ride?" asked Mr. Allen.

Ellen thought she had better act brave even if she didn't feel that way. "I think I'd like the brown one over in the corner of the pen." She thought the brown horse looked gentle.

"I'll take the pinto," said Austine.

"Oh dear," thought Ellen. "I've said the wrong thing. I wish I'd read some horse books."

When the horses were ready, the man who worked at the stables held out his hand, palm up, for Ellen to step into. She put her foot into his hand, and he boosted her onto the horse. The ground seemed a long way below her. Ellen had forgotten how wide a horse was. The man shortened her stirrups and then helped Austine onto the pinto. Ellen patted her horse on the neck. She was anxious to have him like her.

"Look," cried Austine. "I'm really on a horse!"

Ellen knew she was expected to take the lead. "Giddap," she said. The horse did not move.

The man gave each horse a light slap on the rump. They walked out of the corral and down the dirt road as if they were used to going that way. Austine's mother and father followed on foot.

Ellen carefully held one rein in each hand. As she looked at the ground so far below, she hoped the horse wouldn't decide to run.

"I'm going to call my horse Old Paint like in the song," said Austine, who knew about cowboy songs. "Why don't you call yours Brownie?"

"Yes," said Ellen. She didn't feel like talking.

When Austine's horse moved in front, Ellen took hold of the saddle horn. It wasn't so much that she was scared, she told herself. She just didn't want to take any chances.

Maybe this wasn't going to be so bad after all. The horses seemed to know the way, and Ellen found the rocking back and forth to be pleasant. She was even able to look around at the trees and enjoy the woodsy smell.

Then when they had gone around a curve, Brownie wanted to go back to the corral. He turned around and started walking back.

"Hey," said Ellen anxiously. She pulled on the right rein, but Brownie kept on going. "Stop!" she ordered, more loudly this time.

"Why are you going that way?" asked Austine, turning in her saddle.

"Because the horse wants to," said Ellen crossly.

"Well, turn him around."

"I can't," said Ellen. "He won't steer."

Austine turned Old Paint and drew up beside Ellen. "Don't you know you're supposed to hold both reins in one hand?"

Ellen didn't know. "I just held them this way to try to turn him," she said. Ellen took the reins in her left hand.

Austine leaned over and took hold of Brownie's bridle with one hand. "Come on, Old Paint," she said. Brownie followed.

"Thanks," said Ellen. "My, you're brave."

"Oh, that's nothing," said Austine. "You don't steer a horse," she added, "you guide him."

"Oh . . . I forgot." What would Austine think when she found out how Ellen had misled her?

The horses plodded down the road. Through the trees the girls could see the highway and hear cars passing. Austine's mother and father came around the corner, and Ellen began to feel brave again.

"Let's gallop," suggested Austine.

Ellen's legs were beginning to ache. "How do you make them gallop?"

"Dig your heels in," said Austine.

"I wouldn't want to hurt the horse," said Ellen.

"You won't hurt him, silly. Cowboys wear spurs, don't they?"

Ellen timidly kicked Brownie with her heels. Brownie walked slowly on.

Austine dug in her heels. Old Paint began to trot. At first Austine bounced, but soon she rode smoothly. Then her horse began to gallop.

When Old Paint galloped, Brownie began to trot. Ellen began to bounce. She hung onto the saddle horn as hard as she could. Still she bounced. Slap-slap-slap. Her bare legs began to hurt from rubbing against the leather of the saddle flap. Slap-slap-slap. "Goodness, I sound awful," she thought. "I hope Austine doesn't hear me slapping this way."

"Whoa, Old Paint!" cried Austine. Old Paint stopped.

"I did it, Ellen!" she called. "I really, truly galloped. I hung on with my knees and galloped just like in the movies."

"Wh-wh-oa-oa!" Ellen cried. Brownie trotted on. Slap-slap-slap.

Austine began to laugh. "I can see trees between you and the saddle every time you go up. Oh, Ellen, you look so funny!"

Slap-slap-slap. Ellen didn't think she could stand much more bouncing.

"Ellen Tebbits! I don't think you know a thing about horseback riding."

"Wh-wh-oa-oa!" When Brownie reached Old Paint, he stopped. After Ellen got her breath, she cried, "I do, too. It's just that the other horses I rode were tamer."

The horses walked on until the road curved down to the edge of a stream.

"Oh, look. There's a bridge," exclaimed Ellen.

"I guess the highway crosses to the other side of the stream," said Austine. "I wonder if the poor horses would like to drink."

There was no doubt about Brownie's wanting a drink. He left the road and picked his way down the rocky bank to the water. Brownie did not stop at the edge of the stream. He walked out into it.

"Whoa!" yelled Ellen, above the rush of the water. "Austine, help!"

Brownie walked on.

"Austine! What'll I do? He's going swimming!"

"Here, Brownie! Here, Brownie!" called Austine from the bank. Her voice sounded faint across the water.

When Brownie had found his way around the boulders to the middle of the stream, he stopped.

"Look, he's in over his knees!" Ellen looked down at the water. "Giddap, Brownie!"

"Slap him on the rump with the ends of the reins," directed Austine from the bank.

Ellen slapped. Brownie turned his head and looked at her. By this time some hikers had stopped on the bridge. Looking down at Ellen, they laughed and pointed. Ellen wished they would go away.

Brownie lowered his head to drink. Because Ellen had the reins wound around her hand, she could not let go. As she was pulled forward, the saddle horn poked her in the stomach.

"Oof," she said. Hanging over the horse's neck, she clung to his mane with one hand.

Brownie looked at her with water dripping from his chin. Ellen thought it was his chin. Maybe on a horse it was called something else.

A couple of cars stopped on the bridge, and the people looked down at Ellen and laughed. "Do something, Austine," Ellen called. "Our half hour must be nearly up."

"Maybe I could ride back and get the man who owns the horses," Austine yelled back.

"No, Austine. Don't leave me here alone," begged Ellen. "Maybe I could get off. I don't think the water would come up to my shoulders."

"The current's too strong," called Austine. "Anyway, we're supposed to bring the horses back. You can't go off and leave Brownie."

Austine was right. Ellen knew that she couldn't leave Brownie. She might lose him, and the man would probably make her pay for him. She had never heard of anyone losing a horse, so she wasn't sure. "I can't stay here forever," she called.

"Mother and Daddy should catch up with us in a minute," Austine called. "They'll know what to do."

That was just what was worrying Ellen. She didn't want the Allens to see her like this. What would they think after Austine had told them she had ridden before?

One of the hikers climbed down the bank to the edge of the water. "Need some help?" he called.

315

"Oh yes, please," answered Ellen thankfully.

Jumping from boulder to boulder, the man came near her, but he could not get close enough to reach Brownie's bridle. "Throw me the reins," he called.

Ellen threw them as hard as she could. The man grabbed them as the current carried them toward him.

"Come on, old fellow," he said, pulling at the reins. Slowly Brownie began to find his way around the boulders toward the bank.

"Oh, thank you," said Ellen.

"The trouble is, you let the horse know you were afraid of him," said the man. "Let the old nag know you're boss and you won't have any trouble."

"Thank you, I'll try," said Ellen, taking a firm hold on the reins. "Good-bye."

Just then Austine's mother and father came around the corner in the road. "It's time to turn back now," said Mrs. Allen.

"All right, Mother," said Austine. The girls headed their horses toward the corral. Ellen felt bad and she didn't know what to say to Austine. What would Austine think of her after she knew Ellen had exaggerated? What would Austine tell her parents? What would she tell the kids at school?

Finally, Ellen said in a low voice, "I guess I didn't

know quite as much about horseback riding as I thought I did."

"Your horse was just hard to handle, that's all," said Austine.

"Austine?" said Ellen timidly.

"What?"

"You won't tell anybody, will you?"

Austine smiled at her. "Of course I won't tell. We're best friends, aren't we? It'll be our secret. Giddap, Old Paint."

"Thank you," said Ellen. "You're a wonderful friend. You know what? I'm going to look for horse books the next time we go to the library."

If you want to find out more about Ellen and Austine, read Ellen Tebbits *by Beverly Cleary.*

1. What lesson does Ellen learn in this story?

2. What trouble does Ellen have when she and Austine go horseback riding?

3. How does Ellen get Brownie out of the stream?

4. Do you think Austine is a good best friend? Why?

5. How did you know that Austine wouldn't have any trouble with horseback riding?

In "Ellen Rides Again," the character of Ellen changes. In the first part of the story, she is proud and feels very good about herself. Later in the story, she does not feel very good about herself.

Below are four sentences from the story. Tell how you think Ellen felt about herself when each sentence was said.

1. "Oh, yes," said Ellen casually. "Several times."

2. "I've said the wrong thing. I wish I'd read some horse books."

3. "I guess I didn't know quite as much about horseback riding as I thought I did."

4. "Oh, any kind," said Ellen, who did not know one saddle from another.

Now find another sentence in the story that tells about Ellen's character. Be ready to read it to the class.

Thinking About "Milestones"

You read about many people who met milestones in their lives. Some were historical milestones. Remember how Sally and her family traveled to a new place? Think how hard it must have been for someone as shy as Eleanor Roosevelt to begin making speeches for her husband. Through courage and strength these characters were able to do something good for others.

Other characters met personal milestones. After much worry and many unhappy times, Michael finally found the family he always wanted. Ellen Tebbits learned the hard way that she should not mislead her best friend.

The authors of these stories made each of the characters take action. They showed how changes in the characters' lives caused certain results to happen. Each character in this unit faced a problem and reached a milestone. In other stories that you read, decide what milestones the characters reach and how their lives change as a result.

1. The theme of "Milestones" is the reaching of an important point in someone's life. Which characters in this unit faced a historical milestone?

2. What goal did Mike and Michael have in common?

3. Which character in these stories do you think showed the most courage? Explain why you think so.

4. What character do you think showed the most unusual quality? Explain why you think so.

5. Explain how Austine and Cam are alike. Explain how they are different.

Read on Your Own

My Village, Sturbridge by Gary Bowen. Farrar. This book shows what it was like to live in a New England village in the early 1800's.

Ramona and Her Father by Beverly Cleary. Morrow. Ramona's family has to make some changes when her father loses his job.

The Story of Paul Bunyan by Barbara Emberley. Prentice-Hall. This is a tall tale about the famous lumberjack who is as gentle as he is strong. The book tells about some of the amazing adventures he has with his trusty ox, Babe.

The Boy Who Wanted a Family by Shirley Gordon. Harper. This book is about the experiences of a boy and his new mother during the year he is waiting to be adopted. A part of this book appears in this unit.

John Henry: An American Legend by Ezra Jack Keats. Pantheon. This is a tall tale about the man who was "born with a hammer in his hand." He challenges the new steam drill to a contest of power.

How It Feels to Be Adopted by Jill Krementz. Knopf. This book has interviews with adopted children and their adoptive families, who talk about their feelings.

Aaron's Door by Miska Miles. Little, Brown. A young boy has trouble getting used to the idea of being adopted and having a new mother and father.

Adoption by Elaine Scott. Watts. This book discusses adoption, as well as how we are affected by our environment and our family background.

Encyclopedia Brown Shows the Way by Donald J. Sobol. Bantam. A boy detective solves ten crimes in this book. The solutions to the crimes are at the end of the book.

The Adopted One by Sara Stein. Walker. This book is about the feelings of an adopted child. It includes two parts: one for adults to read, and the other for children to read.

Glossary

The glossary is a special dictionary for this book. The glossary tells you how to spell a word, how to pronounce it, and what the word means. Often the word is used in a sentence. Different forms of the word may follow the sentence. If one of the different forms is used in the book, then that form is used in the sentence.

A blue box ■ at the end of the entry tells you that an illustration is given for that word.

The following abbreviations are used throughout the glossary: *n.,* noun; *v.,* verb; *adj.,* adjective; *adv.,* adverb; *interj.,* interjection; *prep.,* preposition; *conj.,* conjunction; *pl.,* plural; *sing.,* singular.

An accent mark (´) is used to show which syllable receives the most stress. For example, in the word *granite* [gran´ it], the first syllable receives the most stress. Sometimes in words of three or more syllables, there is also a lighter mark to show that a syllable receives a lighter stress. For example, in the word *helicopter* [hel´ ə ·kop´ tər], the first syllable has the most stress, and the third syllable has lighter stress.

The symbols used to show how each word is pronounced are explained in the "Pronunciation Key" on the next page.

Pronunciation Key*

a	add, map	m	move, seem	u	up, done
ā	ace, rate	n	nice, tin	û(r)	burn, term
â(r)	care, air	ng	ring, song	yo͞o	fuse, few
ä	palm, father	o	odd, hot	v	vain, eve
b	bat, rub	ō	open, so	w	win, away
ch	check, catch	ô	order, jaw	y	yet, yearn
d	dog, rod	oi	oil, boy	z	zest, muse
e	end, pet	ou	pout, now	zh	vision, pleasure
ē	equal, tree	o͝o	took, full	ə	the schwa,
f	fit, half	o͞o	pool, food		an unstressed
g	go, log	p	pit, stop		vowel representing
h	hope, hate	r	run, poor		the sound spelled
i	it, give	s	see, pass		a in *above*
ī	ice, write	sh	sure, rush		e in *sicken*
j	joy, ledge	t	talk, sit		i in *possible*
k	cool, take	th	thin, both		o in *melon*
l	look, rule	t̶h̶	this, bathe		u in *circus*

*The Pronunciation Key and the short form of the key that appears on the following right-hand pages are reprinted from the *HBJ School Dictionary,* copyright © 1985 by Harcourt Brace Jovanovich, Inc.

A

accept [ak·sept′] *v.* To take something given: He can *accept* small gifts.

ache [āk] *v.* To hurt with a dull pain: Her leg started to *ache* after she fell.

amuse [ə·myōōz′] *v.* To make happy: The clown *amused* the children. **amused**

argue [är′gyōō] *v.* To not agree: The children *argued* about who would get the last piece of apple. **argued**

armchair [ärm′châr′] *n.* A chair with places on each side for people to rest their arms. ■

astronomer [ə·stron′ə·mər] *n.* A person who studies the stars and planets: *Astronomers* may work at night. *pl.* **astronomers**

astronomy [ə·stron′ə·mē] *n.* The study of the stars and planets.

B

barb [bärb] *n.* A point: The *barbs* on the plant caught on his clothes. *pl.* **barbs**

beeswax [bēz′waks] *n.* A word sometimes used in place of the word *business*: None of your *beeswax*!

beet [bēt] *n.* The root of a plant which is used as food: The *beet* added red color to the meal. ■

blossom [blos′əm] **1** *n.* Flower: The *blossoms* were red and pink. **2** *v.* To have flowers: The trees *blossomed* in the spring. *pl.* **blossoms**

blur [blûr] *n.* Something that is not clear: All we saw of the plane was a *blur* as it flew by.

blurt [blûrt] *v.* To say without thinking: He *blurted* out that the horse had run away. **blurted**

bonnet [bon′it] *n.* Hat: The girls in the parade wore white *bonnets. pl.* **bonnets** ■

bother [both′ər] *v.* To make trouble: The dog was *bothering* the cat. **bothering**

bravery [brā′vər·ē] *n.* Courage: The newspaper told about the fire fighter's *bravery.*

burr [bûr] *n.* The head of a flower that has sharp points: The cat got a *burr* in her tail.

busy [biz′ē] **1** *adj.* Working, filled with work: It was a *busy* day. **2** *adv.* In a hard-working way: He *busily* put the books in boxes. **busily**

———— C ————

cabbage [kab′ij] *n.* A vegetable with round, green heads: The *cabbages* grew in rows in the garden. *pl.* **cabbages**

casual [kazh′oo·əl] *adj.* Without plan: He painted the picture *casually.* **casually,** *adv.*

cellar [sel′ər] *n.* A room or rooms under a house: Mother keeps the vegetables in the *cellar.*

clam [klam] *n.* A softbodied sea animal having a shell. We bought *clams* at the store near the ocean. *pl.* **clams**

clatter [klat′ər] *n.* A clashing noise: The *clatter* of the tools kept me awake all night.

coconut [kō′kə·nut′] *n.* Fruit of a tree that grows in warm places. ■

comb [kōm] *n.* A strip of metal or plastic with teeth that is used to care for hair: He carries a *comb* in his pocket.

comet [kom′it] *n.* Bright body in space that moves around the sun: Many *comets* have long tails. *pl.* **comets**

a	add	o	odd	oi	oil
ā	ace	ō	open	ou	pout
â	care	ô	order	ng	ring
ä	palm	ŏŏ	took	th	thin
e	end	ōō	pool	th	this
ē	equal	u	up	zh	vision
i	it	û	burn		
ī	ice	yōō	fuse		

ə = { a in *above*   e in *sicken*   i in *possible*
     o in *melon*   u in *circus* }

community [kə·myoo′nə·tē] *n.* A group of people living near each other: There are many small *communities* near a large city. *pl.* **communities**

continue [kən·tin′yoo] *v.* To go on: He will *continue* his climb after he rests.

cottage [kot′ij] *n.* A small house. ■

crab [krab] *n.* A sea animal having a flat shell: A *crab* walks from side to side.

creative [krē·ā′tiv] *adj.* Having the power to make something new: His *creative* stories made us laugh.

creep [krēp] *v.* To move with the body close to the ground: He *crept* over the grass to the house. **crept**

crew [kroo] *n.* A group of people who work together: All the people on the boat were part of the *crew*.

cucumber [kyoo′kum·bər] *n.* A long green vegetable. We ate the *cucumber* from her father's garden.

current [kûr′ənt] *n.* A part of water that moves in a direction. *pl.* **currents**

cylinder [sil′in·dər] *n.* A part of a machine: The *cylinders* help the machine to run. *pl.* **cylinders**

D

dandelion [dan′də·lī′ən] *n.* A yellow flower: The *dandelion* turned white when it went to seed.

deed [dēd] *n.* An act: Many towns will give an award to someone who performs a brave *deed*.

delight [di·līt′] *n.* Joy: She cried with *delight* when she opened the box.

demand [di·mand′] *v.* To ask in a strong way: Mother *demanded* that we clean our room. **demanded**

depress [di·pres′] *v.* To make sad or gloomy: It was *depressing* to have five days of rain. **depressing,** *adj.*

describe [di·skrīb′] *v.* To tell things about: He *described* the places they had seen on their trip. **described**

description [di·skrip′shən] *n.* Things that tell how something or someone looks: The detective asked the man for a *description* of the car.

dew [d(y)o͞o] *n.* Drops of water that form overnight on grass and trees.

distant [dis′tənt] *adj.* Far away: They will hear a radio program from a *distant* land.

dozen [duz′ən] *n.* A set of twelve: We picked *dozens* of apples today. *pl.* **dozens**

driftwood [drift′wo͝od′] *n.* Wood washed up on the beach: The store showed pretty things made from *driftwood.* ■

dummy [dum′ē] *n.* Something made to look like the real thing: He made a *dummy* of the page before he added the pictures. ■

duty [d(y)o͞o′tē] *n.* A job a person should do: It was my *duty* to make the fire every morning.

E

equal [ē′kwəl] **1** *v.* To do or be the same as: He thinks he can *equal* my time in the race. **2** *adj.* The same as: Mother cut *equal* pieces of meat for the boys.

a	add	o	odd	oi	oil
ā	ace	ō	open	ou	pout
â	care	ô	order	ng	ring
ä	palm	o͝o	took	th	thin
e	end	o͞o	pool	th	this
ē	equal	u	up	zh	vision
i	it	û	burn		
ī	ice	yo͞o	fuse		

ə =	{	a in *above*	e in *sicken*	i in *possible*
		o in *melon*	u in *circus*	

examine [ig·zam'in] *v.* To look at with care: The doctor *examined* the cut on the girl's foot. **examined**

experiment [ik·sper'ə·ment'] *v.* To try out: I will *experiment* with a new kind of paint when I make the dog house.

explode [ik·splōd'] *v.* To burst: The car *exploded* after the fire started. **exploded**

flyspeck [flī'spek'] *n.* A tiny spot: Even a *flyspeck* would show up on her white dress.

fountain [foun'tən] *n.* A stream of water pushing up into the air: The *fountains* in the garden were a beautiful sight. *pl.* **fountains**

freight [frāt] *n.* Goods sent on a train, plane, truck, or ship: The *freight* was sent to the city on a train.

F

fair [fâr] **1** *n.* A place where people show things they use or make: Betty liked to go to the *fair.* **2** *adj.* Being equal for everyone: He wanted to be *fair* to all. **3** *adj.* Beautiful: She thought she was the *fairest.* **fairest**

faucet [fô'sit] *n.* A handle used to turn water on and off: She found the right tool to fix the dripping *faucet.* ■

G

gain [gān] *v.* To go faster or get more: He found he was *gaining* speed as he ran down the hill. **gaining**

gallop [gal'əp] *v.* To run fast: He *galloped* back to the farm. **galloped**

garage [gə·räzh'] *n.* A place where cars are kept. ■

giddap [gid′ap] *v.* A command to a horse to go ahead: *"Giddap,"* she said to the horse to make it move.

glance [glans] *v.* To look at quickly: She just *glanced* at the pictures in the book. **glanced**

gloomy [gloo′mē] *adj.* Sad: She looked at the rain *gloomily*. **gloomily,** *adv.*

glory [glôr′ē] *n.* Beauty: The prize flower was a *glory* to see.

goodness [good′nis] **1** *interj.* A word to show surprise: "My *goodness,* what a big dog!" **2** *n.* A way of being kind or helping others: Her *goodness* made people like her.

great-aunt [grāt′ant′] *n.* An aunt of your mother or father.

gruff [gruf] *adj.* Harsh, growling: He talked with a *gruff* voice.

H

harmonica [här·mon′i·kə] *n.* A small wind instrument: A *harmonica* can be carried in the player's pocket.

harpoon [här·poon′] *n.* A special kind of spear used to catch large sea animals: The *harpoon* on the fishing boat was tied to a rope. ■

headland [hed′lənd] *n.* High land near a body of water: As the boat came around the *headlands* the sailors saw the beach. *pl.* **headlands**

heavenly [hev′ən·lē] *adj.* In space: The closest *heavenly* body to the earth is the moon.

herb [(h)ûrb] *n.* A plant used to make food taste good. *pl.* **herbs**

hermit crab [hûr′mit krab] *n.* A sea animal that lives in the empty shells of other animals.

a	add	o	odd	oi	oil
ā	ace	ō	open	ou	pout
â	care	ô	order	ng	ring
ä	palm	ŏŏ	took	th	thin
e	end	ōō	pool	th	this
ē	equal	u	up	zh	vision
i	it	û	burn		
ī	ice	yōō	fuse		

ə = { a in *above*, e in *sicken*, i in *possible*, o in *melon*, u in *circus* }

hire [hīr] *v.* To agree to pay money for work or use: The family *hired* a man to work in the garden. **hired**

hollow [hol′ō] *n.* A valley: The green *hollows* were beautiful in the spring. *pl.* **hollows**

humdrum [hum′drum] *adj.* Of little interest: It was a *humdrum* play that put the audience to sleep.

I

---

industry [in′dəs·trē] *n.* A business: The town grew when new *industries* opened. *pl.* **industries**

iron [ī′ərn] *n.* A strong metal: The fire did not get past the *iron* door.

item [ī′təm] *n.* Any one thing in a group: She put out all the *items* she needed to make the meal. *pl.* **items**

ivy [ī′vē] *n.* A green climbing plant: The *ivy* has covered our fence.

K

---

kazoo [kə·zoo′] *n.* A small instrument played by humming into it: There was special music for the *kazoo* in the band. ■

L

---

language [lang′gwij] *n.* The words used by groups of people to talk to each other: My sister has learned three *languages* in school. *pl.* **languages**

length [leng(k)th] *n.* The measure from end to end: He ran the *length* of the field.

lie [lī] *v.* **1** To rest as on a bed: I felt like *lying* down until dinner. **2** To say something that is not true: She was *lying* about her job. **lying**

lifeboat [līf′bōt′] *n.* A small boat to use if there is trouble on a big ship: The people got into the *lifeboat*.

lilac [lī′lak′] *n.* A large shrub with sweet-smelling flowers that are usually purple or white.

locomotive [lō′kə·mō′tiv] *n.* An engine that pulls a train: His father drives a *locomotive.*

M

---

mane [mān] *n.* Long hair around the neck of an animal: She held onto the horse's *mane.* ■

memory [mem′ər·ē] *n.* The act of remembering: He kept the names and numbers in his *memory.*

mineral [min′ər·əl] *n.* A thing found naturally in the ground that is not a plant or an animal: They wanted the land because of the *minerals* in the soil. *pl.* **minerals**

misread [mis·rēd′] *v.* To read in a way that the reader gets the wrong information: If you *misread* the sign, you may take a wrong turn.

mollusk [mol′əsk] *n.* A water animal with a soft body and a hard shell: Some kinds of *mollusks* are very good to eat. *pl.* **mollusks**

mutter [mut′ər] *v.* To say in a low voice: I could hardly hear him *mutter* the answer.

N

---

narrow [nar′ō] *adj.* Not wide: The road to the house was too *narrow* for the truck.

nip [nip] *v.* To bite: The dog was *nipping* at the cat's tail. **nipping**

a	add	o	odd	oi	oil
ā	ace	ō	open	ou	pout
â	care	ô	order	ng	ring
ä	palm	ŏŏ	took	th	thin
e	end	ōō	pool	th	this
ē	equal	u	up	zh	vision
i	it	û	burn		
ī	ice	yōō	fuse		

ə = { a in *above*   e in *sicken*   i in *possible*
 o in *melon*   u in *circus* }

non-living [non′liv′ing] *adj.* Not alive: Rocks are made of a *non-living* material.

O
---

oar [ôr] *n.* A wooden pole used to make a boat move through the water: We moved the boat with the *oars*. *pl.* **oars** ■

obey [ō·bā′] *v.* To do as told: Games are more fun when people *obey* the rules.

orbit [ôr′bit] *n.* A path around something: The picture showed the moon's *orbit*.

P
---

panel [pan′əl] *n.* A board with instruments to run something: She sat at the instrument *panel* of the plane.

parsley [pärs′lē] *n.* An herb whose leaves give a special taste to food: Mother put the *parsley* on the meat.

passenger [pas′ən·jər] *n.* A person who rides on a train, bus, plane, boat, or car: The *passengers* in the plane were given something to eat. *pl.* **passengers**

pause [pôz] *n.* A small stop: When there was a *pause* in the music, someone laughed.

peel [pēl] *v.* To take away the skin: He *peels* oranges before he eats them. *pl.* **peels** ■

peg [peg] *n.* A wooden pin on which someone without a leg may walk: One of the pirate's legs was a *peg*.

photographic [fō′tə·graf′ik] *adj.* Like a photograph: Her *photographic* memory is what helps her remember things.

pirate [pī′rit] *n.* A person who robs ships: The *pirate* took the treasure to the beach.

piston [pis′tən] *n.* A part of a machine that moves up and down in a tube: The machine came to a stop when the *piston* broke.

plead [plēd] *v.* To beg: They *pleaded* for help. **pleaded**

poison [poi′zən] *v.* To put something in food or drink that will hurt or kill: She *poisoned* the snake. **poisoned**

postcard [pōst′kärd] *n.* A card used to send messages through the mail. ■

prepare [prī·pâr′] *v.* To get ready: She *prepares* his lunch for him every other day. **prepares**

pronounce [prə·nouns′] *v.* To say: The book shows how to *pronounce* every word.

pumpkin [pump′kin] *n.* A large orange fruit: We cut a face on the *pumpkin* for Halloween.

Q

queen [kwēn] *n.* A woman who rules a land on her own: The *queen* sat on a very large chair.

R

radish [rad′ish] *n.* A small red vegetable: He cut the *radish* before he ate it.

respect [ri·spekt′] *v.* To show honor: They help by *respecting* what does not belong to them. **respecting**

rhyme [rīm] *n.* Lines in a poem that end with words sounding the same: He writes *rhymes* for birthday cards. *pl.* **rhymes**

ridge [rij] *n.* A long, thin strip: The plow made *ridges* in the soil. *pl.* **ridges**

a	add	o	odd	oi	oil
ā	ace	ō	open	ou	pout
â	care	ô	order	ng	ring
ä	palm	ŏŏ	took	th	thin
e	end	o͞o	pool	th	this
ē	equal	u	up	zh	vision
i	it	û	burn		
ī	ice	yo͞o	fuse		

ə = { a in *above* e in *sicken* i in *possible*
      o in *melon* u in *circus* }

335

S

saddle [sad′(ə)l] *n.* A seat for a rider on a horse: The *saddles* for the horses were on the fence. *pl.* **saddles**

sample [sam′pəl] *n.* A part that shows what the whole thing is like: I gave her a *sample* of the cheese.

sandal [san′dəl] *n.* An open shoe: He wore his *sandals* when he walked on the beach. *pl.* **sandals** ■

satisfaction [sat′is·fak′shən] *n.* The feeling that all is as it should be: The father looked at the boy's work with *satisfaction.*

scatter [skat′ər] *v.* To throw about: She *scatters* food for the birds in her garden. **scatters** ■

sense [sens] *n.* A way through which the body finds out about the world outside: Sight, smell, touch, hearing, and taste are the five *senses*. *pl.* **senses**

serious [sir′ē·əs] *adj.* **1** Thoughtful. **2** Not joking: He was *serious* when he talked about going.

service [sûr′vis] *n.* **1** Things done for others: We are at your *service.* **2** Things done for the people in a town that are paid for by their taxes: The work of the fire fighters is one of the *services* of our city. *pl.* **services**

shrub [shrub] *n.* A bush: The rabbit lived under the *shrub.*

sight [sīt] *n.* The act of seeing: After many days at sea there was a *sighting* star for the sailors to guide them to land. **sighting** *adj.*

sink [singk] *v.* To go down: After the rain the boat *sank.* **sank**

slate [slāt] *n.* A piece of thin rock: The *slates* on the roof were red. *pl.* **slates**

slope [slōp] *v.* To cause to slant: The land *sloped* down to the lake. **sloped**

slouch [slouch] *v.* To walk or stand in a way that is not straight. **slouched**

snail [snāl] *n.* A small slow-moving animal with a shell: He bought a *snail* to help keep the fish bowl clean.

solar system [sō′lər sis′təm] *n.* The sun and the planets around it. The moon is part of the *solar system.*

sow [sō] *v.* To plant seeds: The farmer needed help *sowing* his corn seeds. **sowing**

spear [spir] *n.* A long pole with a point at the end: The Indians used a *spear* to hunt for animals.

spirit [spir′it] *n.* The life-giving force: The player gave *spirit* to the team.

stable [stā′bəl] *n.* A place where horses are kept. *pl.* **stables**

station [stā′shən] *n.* A place from which trains and buses leave and to which they return: They met me when my bus got to the *station.*

stopper [stop′ər] *n.* Something used to close up a bottle: She used the *stopper* on the bottle to keep the water fresh. ■

sturdy [stûr′dē] *adj.* Strong: We put the treasure in a *sturdy* box.

supply [sə·plī′] *n.* A needed material: The sailors bought *supplies* for the ship. *pl.* **supplies**

sway [swā] *v.* To move from side to side: The tree was *swaying* in the wind. **swaying**

a	add	o	odd	oi	oil
ā	ace	ō	open	ou	pout
â	care	ô	order	ng	ring
ä	palm	o͝o	took	th	thin
e	end	o͞o	pool	th	this
ē	equal	u	up	zh	vision
i	it	û	burn		
ī	ice	yo͞o	fuse		

ə = { a in *above*   e in *sicken*   i in *possible*
        o in *melon*   u in *circus* }

337

T

tear [târ] *v.* To pull apart: The wind was *tearing* the side of the tent open. **tearing**

temper [tem′pər] *n.* A strong feeling: I was in a bad *temper*.

term [tûrm] *n.* A time to hold a job: Her *term* as mayor was four years.

thief [thēf] *n.* Someone who steals: The *thief* took the gold from the store.

time machine [tīm′mə·shēn′] *n.* Something make-believe that could carry people backward or forward in time: Many stories have been written about a *time machine*.

timid [tim′id] *adj.* Shy: She was *timid* when she had to meet new people.

tissue paper [tish′oo·pā′pər] *n.* A thin soft paper: The dress was wrapped in *tissue paper* in the box. ■

trail [trāl] *v.* To fall behind: By the end of the fourth lap, I *trailed* the other runners. **trailed**

transportation [trans′pər·tā′shən] *n.* A way of going from place to place: Trains and planes are two forms of *transportation*.

trot [trot] *v.* To move between a walk and a run. **trotted**

trousers [trou′zərz] *n.* An outer covering for the lower part of the body: He wore a blue coat and white *trousers*. ■

tube [t(y)oob] *n.* Something long, hollow, and round: He joined the bottles with two rubber *tubes*. *pl.* **tubes**

U

upright [up′rīt′] *adv.* On end: He put the pole *upright* in the ground.

upside-down [up'sīd doun] *adj.* With the top part at the bottom: We saw the *upside-down* boat on the beach.

V
---

vine [vīn] *n.* A plant that climbs: The *vines* grew up the side of the house. *pl.* **vines**

W
---

wander [won'dər] *v.* To go off without following a path: She *wandered* all over the park. **wandered**

wheelbarrow [(h)wēl'bar'ō] *n.* Something that has a top like a box and a large wheel on which it rolls when pushed: He took the dirt to the garden in a *wheelbarrow.* ■

whine [(h)wīn] *v.* To cry: The dog *whined* when it wanted to come into the house. **whined**

whip [(h)wip] *v.* To pull out fast: He *whipped* his car out onto the road. **whipped**

wicked [wik'id] *adj.* Very bad: The *wicked* man took the girl's treasure.

woodsy [wŏŏd'zē] *adj.* Of the woods: There was a *woodsy* smell near the cabin.

wreck [rek] *n.* Something ruined: The car was a *wreck* after the accident.

wrestle [res'(ə)l] *n.* An exercise in which one person forces another's body or arm to the ground or a table: Our team made *wrestling* look easy. **wrestling**

a	add	o	odd	oi	oil
ā	ace	ō	open	ou	pout
â	care	ô	order	ng	ring
ä	palm	ŏŏ	took	th	thin
e	end	ōō	pool	th	this
ē	equal	u	up	zh	vision
i	it	û	burn		
ī	ice	yōō	fuse		

ə = { a in *above*   e in *sicken*   i in *possible*
      o in *melon*   u in *circus* }

Word List

The following words are introduced in this book. Each is listed beside the number of the page in which it first appears.

The Shoemaker's Gift
(4–13)

4   leather
5   surrounded
6   grants
7   chambers
8   request
     secretary
9   entrance
11   messenger
     fetch
     arrived
     presence

The Travels of Marco Polo
(16–21)

16   Marco Polo
     Venice
     Nicolò
     Maffeo
     Kublai Khan
17   Israel
     camels
     Armenia
18   Peking
     carved
     marble
     Persia
     Iran

19   spices
     Java
     Sumatra
     Rustichello
     A Description of the World
     Christopher Columbus
     Spain

Sequence
(22–25)

22   time order
23   Mayflower
     Plymouth
24   supplies
     Hannibal Bridge
     Missouri River
     passage
     phrase
     area
25   industries
     transportation
     oars
     iron

Molly's Pilgrim
(26–35)

26   Molly
     Pilgrims

     assignment
     Jewish
     Russia
     Miss Stickley
27   Nu
     shaynkeit
     Malkeleh
     religious
28   arithmetic
     embroidered
     felt
     kerchief
     gorgeous
     managed
     satisfied
30   aisles
     taunted
31   magnificent
     Polish
32   Sukkos
     announced
33   Emma

Diagrams
(36–37)

36   caption
     additional
37   locomotive
     boiler
     cylinders
     piston

341

Key: (l)-Left; (r)-Right; (c)-Center; (b)-Bottom

Photographs

Cover: © 1965 California Institute of Technology; (insert) HBJ Photo; NASA.

Page 2–3, HBJ Photo/John Petrey; 38–39, Jim Shaughnessy; 41, Jim Shaughnessy; 74, HBJ Photo/John Petrey; 78, Kurt Scholz/Shostal; 79(l), Ken Scholz/Shostal; 79(r), Fritz Henle/Photo Researchers; 106–107, Vandystadt/Photo Researchers; 151, Kurt Scholz/Shostal 154–155, HBJ Photo/Paul Gerding; 196–197, Larry Lefever/Grant Heilman; 200, Rafael Macia/Photo Researchers; 202(t), W.H. Hodge/Peter Arnold; 202(b), A&Z Collection Ltd./Photo Researchers; 203(t), Courtesy of W. Atlas Burpee Co.; 203(b), Ed Simpson/After Image; 204, Robert M. Friedman/Frozen Images; 205(t), Jon Yeager/Photo Library; 205(b), Robert P. Carr/Bruce Coleman; 206, HBJ Photo/Rodney Jones; 207, Russ Kinne/Photo Researchers; 208(t), W.H. Hodge/Peter Arnold; 208(b), C.C. Lockwood/Bruce Coleman; 209(t), Ken Brate/Photo Researchers; 209(b), HBJ Photo/Rodney Jones; 228, HBJ Photo/Paul Gerding; 232 (top to bottom), Brown Brothers, Bechtold/Stock Shop, Granger Collection, Tommy Thompson/Stills, Inc., Brown Brothers, Grant Heilman, NASA, Brown Brothers; 233(l), Bettmann Archive; 233(c), H. Armstrong Roberts; 233(r), Comstock, Inc.; 243, Robert S. Arnold; 244, Robert S. Arnold; 245, Robert S. Arnold, 321, Grant Heilman.

Contents: Unit 1, 2–3, HBJ Photo/John Petrey; Unit 2, 78, Ken Sholz/Shostal; Unit 3, 154–155, HBJ Photo/Paul Gerding; Unit 4, 233, H. Armstrong Roberts.

Illustrators

Lynn Adams: 22–25, 94–95, 112–125; Dave Blanchette: 262–263, 282–283, 294–299; Valerie Brachman: 14–15; Jesse Clay: 171–177; Susan David: 284–290; Marie DeJohn: 304–317; Dee Deloy: 16–17, 249; Lane DuPont: 142–147; Leslie Dunlap: 56–63, 272; Larry Frederick: 276–279; Wayne Hovis: 52–53, 198; Robert Korta: 180–183; Barbara Lanza: 326–339; Kaaren Lewis: 132–133; Gary Lippencott: 264–269; The Marketing Connection, Florida: 166–167; Al Michini: 18, 44–49, 260–261; Monica Santa: 54, 168–169, 251–256; Steven Schindler: 4–11; John Walter, Jr.: 36–37; James Watling: 66–71; John Weecks: 234–239; Michelle Wiggins: 134–139; Lane Yerkes: 184–193.

7
C 8
D 9
E 0
F 1
G 2
H 3
I 4
J 5